Newcomers in American Schools

Meeting the Educational Needs of Immigrant Youth

Lorraine M. McDonnell, Paul T. Hill

Supported by the
Andrew W. Mellon Foundation

RAND

During the 1980s, the largest and most diverse group of immigrants arrived in the United States since the beginning of the century. These growing numbers of immigrants are having profound effects on the urban areas where they concentrate and on the institutions called upon to assist them and their children to adjust and participate fully in the country's economic, social, and political life.

This report focuses on the responses of arguably the most important of these institutions: the schools. It assesses the federal and state roles in immigrant education, describes how school districts are responding, and offers suggestions for improving immigrant education. The report is intended for a broad audience with an interest in education and in immigration issues, including public policymakers, state and local officials, the education community, and academic researchers.

The project was funded by the Mellon Foundation and by the Program for Research on Immigration Policy. The latter, created in February 1988, first focused on assessing the implementation and effects of the Immigration Reform and Control Act of 1986. It then began to study the larger, continuing questions of integration of immigrants into the economic, social, and political life of the country and to assess the demands immigrants are placing on our institutions, including schools, postsecondary educational institutions, and local governments. The program also has examined the link between immigration and key foreign and international policy issues associated with a potential North American Economic Integration and with the fundamental changes brought about by European integration and the liberalization and restructuring in Eastern Europe and the former Soviet Union.

The program also disseminates and exchanges information concerning immigration and immigrant policies. Researchers interested in receiving program publications or in attending its working groups and conferences should address inquiries to:

Georges Vernez
Director, Program for Research on Immigration Policy
RAND
1700 Main Street
P.O. Box 2138
Santa Monica, CA 90407-2138
Telephone: (310) 393-0411

CONTENTS

TABLES

The United States is now experiencing a wave of immigration unprecedented since the early 1900s, with the most recent Census showing that nine million people emigrated here during the 1980s. The more than two million immigrant youth who enrolled in U.S. public schools over the past decade represent significant challenges for local school systems. Like earlier waves of immigrant students, most are concentrated in a few large cities; they are typically poor; many have suffered the traumas of war, civil strife, or economic deprivation; and all must learn the language and customs of a new country. But recent newcomers hail from a more diverse range of cultures than earlier groups, which were primarily European.

Despite the significant numbers of immigrant students now entering U.S. schools, their unique needs are only dimly recognized by federal and state policymakers. Those who are most aware of these students are the educators who work in the local districts where most immigrants are concentrated. These teachers and administrators express optimism about their ability to educate immigrant children and to integrate them successfully into American life. But their efforts are largely ad hoc, dependent on the willingness and ability of individual educators, rather than the result of concerted policy initiatives.

STUDY PURPOSE AND METHODS

In this report, we examine the schooling needs of immigrant students, assess how well these needs are currently being met, and suggest strategies for improving schooling outcomes for immigrants.

The study analyzed immigrant education from a broad policy perspective, explicitly considering it as a political issue in competition for policymakers' attention and scarce public resources and as one of many challenges facing increasingly overburdened local school systems.

Although it is difficult conceptually and politically to separate an analysis of the education of immigrant students from current controversies surrounding U.S. immigration policy, the two should be viewed as separate issues. Whatever one thinks about the need for new immigration laws or stricter enforcement of existing ones, that dispute is distinct from the education of children already living in the United States. The humane reason is that these are innocent children who are in this country because of adult actions over which they have little control and who deserve the attention a caring society accords all its children. The utilitarian reason is that these children are literally the nation's future. Most of them will remain here as adults, and the quality of education they receive will shape the quality of life all Americans enjoy over the next several decades—they are tomorrow's citizens and workers.

Study data were collected from a purposive sample of nine school districts and 57 schools, chosen to reflect the range of communities in which immigrant children now live. Six districts—New York, Los Angeles, Chicago, Miami, Houston, and San Francisco—were selected because together they enroll the overwhelming majority of immigrant students nationally. Visalia, California (a rural district), and Fairfax County, Virginia (a suburban district), were included because they are typical of nonurban districts that have experienced large influxes of immigrant students in recent years. On-site and telephone interviews were conducted with 240 district and school administrators, teachers, counselors, and community representatives. To supplement the statistical and interview data and obtain a systematic portrait of immigrant schooling experiences, the transcripts of 745 students enrolled in six Los Angeles schools were coded and analyzed. In addition, 38 interviews were conducted with state-level policymakers (governors' education aides, legislators, state department of education staff, and interest-group representatives) in the six states in which the sample districts are located.

MAJOR CONCLUSIONS

Four major conclusions emerge from this research:

1. Although they represent only a fraction of the nation's youth, immigrants constitute a growing proportion of that cohort and are heavily concentrated in a few areas of the country.

Seventy-eight percent of all immigrant students who have been in the United States for three years or less attend school in just five states, with 45 percent enrolled in California. As of 1990, 11 percent of all youth living in California were born outside the United States; the proportions for New York, Florida, Texas, and Illinois range between 6 and 3 percent. Together, these five states are home to over 1.5 million immigrant youth. In the large city school districts of Los Angeles and Miami, immigrant students represent 20 percent of the total enrollment.

2. Immigrant education is not a visible policy issue. Independent of their need to learn English and to escape the consequences of poverty, immigrant students are not viewed by federal and state policymakers as a distinct group requiring unique policy remedies. That immigrants may have different needs than native-born students is not widely recognized nor accepted.

Because the costs and potential benefits from immigration fall overwhelmingly on a few states and local districts, most notably in California, the rest of the country has little incentive to concern itself with the education of immigrants. The role that the federal government plays in the schooling of immigrant students is limited. At a programmatic level, it functions as a junior partner, funding several small categorical programs that pay parts of the costs borne by states and local districts. The federal government exerts its greatest impact on immigrant education through regulation: Federal judicial decisions and civil rights enforcement have created a framework that defines the legal rights of limited-English proficiency (LEP) students, including most immigrants. Similarly, the education of immigrant children is not a definable policy issue at the state level. Most states have policies and programs for LEP students, but these were developed to meet the needs of American-born speakers of foreign languages (e.g., Puerto Ricans in New York), not immigrants. The needs and problems of immigrant students are rarely considered independent of their status as non-English speakers. In state policymaking, immigrant education is equated with bilingual education, and it therefore bears all the emotional baggage left over from divisive debates about bilingual education and native-language maintenance. Immigrant students' other needs, derived from their status as newcomers who have fled poor and war-torn areas, are seldom recognized.

3. The quality of schooling that immigrant students receive largely depends on the capacity of the local communities in which they reside. Yet most of these districts and schools lack the human and fiscal resources to educate students well, whether they are immigrant or native-born.

With very few exceptions, the teachers and administrators who serve immigrant children do so with care and enthusiasm. Nevertheless, the school districts serving the largest numbers of immigrant students are deeply troubled and frequently fail to provide high-quality educational services to students of all sorts, including native-born, low- and middle-income children, as well as immigrants. Big-city school districts lack the assets normally considered necessary for the education of language-minority students. Although a few have adequate supplies of Spanish-speaking teachers, none can guarantee that immigrants speaking other languages will be taught by bilingual teachers. These districts also lack appropriate instructional materials and can do little for the increasing numbers of older immigrant students who arrive having had little formal schooling in their native countries. Few schools have routine, easy access to the educational, health, and social support services desperately needed by students who must cope with the effects of poverty and the traumas associated with leaving one culture and adjusting to another.

Policymakers and academics continue to debate whether bilingual education should be primarily a vehicle for teaching students English or whether it should provide an ongoing link to their native language and culture. However, in most school districts enrolling large numbers of immigrant students, the logic of necessity overwhelms either side of that debate. In general, school systems offer at least some bilingual education to new immigrant students whenever possible. But the needs of students who speak no English are so great and the instructional resources so scarce that few districts are able to offer any native-language instruction to those who are even moderately competent in English.

Despite the unique needs of immigrant students, however, many of the service gaps they experience also adversely affect U.S.-born students. These stem from the current condition of big-city school districts—their inability to cope with growing fiscal deficits, facility overcrowding, shortages of qualified teachers, and weak links to other community institutions. Large urban districts are failing to educate a high proportion of their students—nearly half drop out before graduation in some cities—and some of the larger districts are unable to ensure the safety of students and teachers while in school.

4. Immigrant students have unmet educational needs that are unique to their newcomer status. But the best way to help immigrant students is to strengthen the school systems that serve them, not to create new categorical programs that single out immigrants for special benefits.

The quality of immigrant education depends on the fundamental strength and competence of big-city school systems. The financial and educational weaknesses of those school systems impede any effort to improve schooling for immigrant children. Certainly, strategies need to be promoted that are specific to improving the educational outcomes of immigrant students. However, the most effective way to improve schooling for immigrant students is to enhance the overall capacity of urban school systems.

Although current educational reform proposals can help strengthen urban schools, they do not go far enough. They assume that school systems have the resources necessary to improve their own performance, if only efforts are properly focused by means of goals, standards, and accountability measures. School systems that are beset by debt, declining and unstable revenues, dilapidated buildings, and inadequate instructional resources cannot improve simply by trying harder.

Some way must be found for the federal government and states to move beyond their current emphasis on small categorical programs to help big cities improve their school systems across the board. This effort needs to engage a broad range of private- and public-sector institutions, and continued assistance should be contingent on school performance, but it must happen. Immigrant students and their urban schoolmates constitute a key segment of the country's future economic and social life. If their opportunities for a productive and satisfying life are not significantly enhanced, the consequences will be felt far beyond the five states where most immigrants now live.

ACKNOWLEDGMENTS

Completing a project of this scope requires a variety of different skills, and we were fortunate in being able to draw on the talents of a number of people. Margaret Camarena, Lin Liu, Beth Lewis, Kathy Rosenblatt, and Kelly Warner assisted us in collecting the field and telephone interview data. Marilyn Gerbi and Kathy Rosenblatt compiled and coded all the student transcripts. Tor Ormseth and Jeannette Van Winkle assisted in analyzing the transcript data.

Throughout this project, Stephanie Bell-Rose and Juliet Ofori of the Mellon Foundation provided support through their efforts to create and sustain discussions among a variety of researchers working on different aspects of immigration policy and the immigrant experience. This report benefited from the thoughtful reviews of Ruben Carriedo of the San Diego City Schools and Michael Fix of the Urban Institute. Although their suggestions for interpreting and presenting material were particularly useful, they are in no way responsible for the report's conclusions or shortcomings.

Marilyn Gerbi's efforts in preparing this manuscript are much appreciated.

Chapter One

INTRODUCTION

In chronicling the history of urban education in the United States, David Tyack (1974) noted that "immigrant children . . . posed the most visible challenge to school people as they went to work in northern cities at the turn of the century" (pp. 239–240). The U.S. Senate Immigration Commission reported in 1908 that students attending school in the nation's 37 largest cities represented over 60 nationalities, and 58 percent of all students had fathers who were born abroad. Between 1900 and 1910, more than eight million immigrants entered this country. That influx of immigrants became a primary force in transforming the organization and curriculum of U.S. public schools in ways that have endured to the present.

The United States is now witnessing a second major wave of immigration, with the 1990 Census showing that nine million people emigrated here during the 1980s. Although the absolute numbers are greater than in the earlier peak period, this wave represents a smaller net increase in population (less than 4 percent, as compared with 10 percent between 1900 and 1910). Nevertheless, the more than two million immigrant youth who enrolled in U.S. public schools over the past decade represent greater challenges for local school systems than did their historical counterparts. Like the earlier wave of immigrant students, most are concentrated in a few large cities; they are typically poor; many have suffered the traumas of war, civil strife, or economic deprivation; and all must learn the language and customs of a new country. But the current group of newcomers hails from a more diverse range of cultures than earlier groups, which came primarily from Europe, and a higher proportion have had little or no formal schooling in their native countries.

Despite the significant numbers of immigrant students now entering U.S. schools, their unique needs are only dimly recognized by federal and state policymakers. Those who are most aware of these students are the educators who work in the local districts where most immigrants are concentrated. Like many of their colleagues of 80 years ago, these teachers and administrators express optimism about their ability to educate immigrant children and to integrate them successfully into American life. But their efforts are largely ad hoc, dependent on the willingness and ability of individual educators, rather than the result of concerted policy initiatives.

This report examines the schooling needs of immigrant students, assesses how well they are currently being met, and suggests strategies for improving schooling outcomes for immigrants. This first chapter presents a summary portrait of the demographic characteristics of immigrant students and what we know about their schooling experiences from past research. The chapter then outlines the study purpose and research methods.

IMMIGRANT STUDENTS: HOW MANY, WHO ARE THEY, WHERE DO THEY LIVE?

The limited visibility of immigrant students is evidenced in the lack of precise estimates of their numbers. To the extent that they have certain other characteristics—limited English-language proficiency, an educational disadvantage, giftedness, a disability—immigrant students are counted as part of these other groups. However, neither the federal government nor individual states count, as a separate group, all those students who were born in other countries.

The most comprehensive and up-to-date information comes from the 1990 Census, which includes counts of all foreign-born youth under age 18. As Table 1.1 indicates, immigrants represent only a small fraction of the nation's youth. However, young immigrants are heavily concentrated in only a few areas of the country, with over 70 percent living in just five states. Particularly notable is the concentration in California, which has become home to a majority of the nation's immigrant youth. Table 1.2 shows the proportion of immigrant youth living in the eight communities included in the study sample for this project (described below). Especially striking is the significant proportion of immigrant youth living in the nation's largest cities, particularly those located in the Sunbelt.

Table 1.1

Concentration of Immigrant Youth in Five States

	Foreign-Born Youth Under 18 Years	As a Percentage of All Foreign-Born Youth in the U.S.	As a Percentage of All Youth in the State
California	852,514	41	11
New York	258,296	12	6
Texas	196,547	9	4
Florida	144,748	7	5
Illinois	87,122	4	3

SOURCE: 1990 Census of Population and Housing, U.S. Census Bureau.
NOTE: In the United States overall, there were 2,092,460 foreign-born youth under 18, constituting 3 percent of all youth under 18.

Table 1.2

Immigrant Youth in Selected U.S. Communities

	Foreign-Born Youth Under 18 Years	Foreign-Born as a Percentage of All Youth Under 18 years
New York City	205,904	12
Los Angeles	184,048	21
Chicago	48,555	7
Dade County (Miami)	85,567	18
Houston	41,488	10
San Francisco	22,745	19
Fairfax County, VA	16,163	8
Visalia, CA	1,824	8

SOURCE: 1990 Census of Population and Housing, U.S. Census Bureau.
NOTE: The figures listed here are for areas that are contiguous with the school districts by the same name. The exception is Los Angeles. These figures are for the city of Los Angeles; the Los Angeles Unified School District extends beyond the city limits to include unincorporated areas and several additional cities, such as Bell, Cudahy, South Gate, and San Pedro.

Although the census data are the most comprehensive, they represent a count of all youth, including those too young to be enrolled in school. The only national count of immigrant students is collected as part of a small federal categorical program targeted to students who have been in the United States for three years or less. Table 1.3

Table 1.3

Immigrant and LEP Students in Five States
(1989–1990)

	Immigrant Students in the U.S. Three Years or Less[a]	Students Identified as LEP
California	268,455	861,531
Florida	18,697	61,768
Illinois	30,965	73,185
New York	100,769	158,007
Texas	47,963	309,862
U.S. Total	602,178	2,154,781

SOURCE: U.S. Department of Education (1991).

[a]The figures in this column underestimate the number of students who have resided in the United States for three years or less by approximately 15 percent. These data are only collected for the purpose of allocating federal funds, and program eligibility criteria restrict funding to only those districts with a minimal concentration of recent immigrants. Therefore, not all recent immigrants are included in this count.

shows that 78 percent of all recent immigrant students attend school in just five states, with 45 percent enrolled in California. Table 1.3 also shows the number of students who were identified in 1989 as having limited proficiency in English. Although the overwhelming majority of limited-English-proficient (LEP) students are immigrants, the LEP count is not a perfect proxy for the number of immigrant students, because LEP students from Puerto Rico are included in this count, although they are not considered immigrants, while immigrant students from English-speaking countries are not included in the LEP count.

Immigrant students are a diverse group. For example, in 1989, New York reported that immigrant students who had been in the United States for three years or less came from 162 different countries. In 1990, California reported that LEP students in the state spoke 46 different primary languages. But amidst this diversity are important similarities. Just as the overwhelming majority of immigrant students and their families have chosen to settle in only a few areas of the United States, most have emigrated from only a few regions of the world. The vast majority of immigrant students come from Spanish-speaking countries in Central and South America. For example, Spanish is the primary language of 76 percent of LEP students in California, and the proportion is similar in the other large immigrant states. Another major source is Asia. About 17 percent of LEP students in California speak one of nine Asian languages. The proportion of recent immigrants in New York state who are Asian is about the same as in California (16 percent). Other countries sending significant numbers of immigrant students to the United States are those in Eastern Europe and the former Soviet Union.

PAST RESEARCH

Despite the growing presence of immigrant students in the nation's largest cities and states, research about their schooling experience is limited.[1] With a few notable exceptions (e.g., Caplan, et al., 1991), most of the research is ethnographic. Studies tend to focus on the educational and adjustment experiences of particular immigrant groups—e.g., Sikhs in a rural California town (Gibson, 1988), Central American immigrants in two inner-city high schools (Suárez-Orozco, 1989), the children of Southeast Asian refugees in five sites across the country (Caplan, et al., 1991), and high-achieving Mexican immigrants in a midwestern, urban high school (Duran and Weffer, 1992).

Three major findings emerge from these studies. First, they document the adjustment problems that immigrant students face. These stem from the need to learn a new language; to deal with possible disruptions to family life if immigrant children are separated from parents or siblings; to cope with the effects of poverty; and to adjust to a culture that may simultaneously be confusing, threatening, and at odds with the values of an immigrant student's own culture. In reviewing the psychological research literature on Hispanic immigrants Suárez-Orozco and Suárez-Orozco (1993) describe what they call the "immigrant paradox." On the one hand, movement to the United States represents instrumental gains as economic conditions

---

[1]In contrast to the paucity of studies about the contemporary education of immigrants, a number of historians (e.g., Tyack, 1974; Callahan, 1962) have examined the profound effect that immigration at the beginning of the 20th century had on American education. As P. Fass (1989) notes, key elements of the progressive reforms, such as student testing, tracking, and the notion of the common school, were specifically "framed in the light of the complex issues of student heterogeneity and strongly informed by contemporary perceptions about immigrants." There is a general consensus among historians that this influx of immigrants into the public schools, while not the sole reason, was a major impetus for the transformation of schooling from a localistic enterprise to a more uniform, professional, and bureaucratic undertaking.

improve for immigrants and their families. On the other hand, they often suffer deep affective losses as supportive familial and community ties in their native countries are broken, and they lose the support network necessary for psychological well-being. Nevertheless, a review of studies of the adjustment of immigrant children in the United States and other countries concluded that they adjust socially and emotionally no better or worse than the native populations into which they migrate.

When adjustment does result in social and emotional disorders, it most usually takes the form of behavior deviance and, in adolescence, identity conflicts (Aronowitz, 1984).[2]

Second, as Gibson (1988) concludes, there is mounting evidence that immigrant youth do comparatively well in school, especially if they receive most of their education in their new homeland.

> In many cases, they do better academically and persist in school longer than native-born majority-group peers of similar class backgrounds or, frequently, even of the middle class (p. 173).

Although different studies vary in their explanations for this finding, several factors emerge as important. Caplan and his colleagues found that, among the Southeast Asian boat people, values that stress education and achievement, a cohesive family, and hard work were significant in explaining their children's academic achievement. In their study of high-achieving Mexican immigrants, Duran and Weffer (1992) concluded that

> Although the influence of family educational values was not strong enough to affect achievement outcomes, values did influence student behavior at school in an important manner. Values influenced student willingness to take on extra work (p. 179).

---

[2]A more recent ethnographic study by the same author, comparing native-born Jewish children with Soviet emigres attending the same Jewish parochial school in San Francisco, found that parental attitudes toward social change and new experiences were significant predictors of the in-school adjustment of both immigrant and native children, even when family and student characteristics were held constant. Parental attitudes toward social change and new experience were not found to be differentially associated with adjustment for immigrant as opposed to native students (Aronowitz, 1992).

In reviewing past studies and in summarizing her own study of Sikh students, Gibson (1988) notes that most teachers like teaching immigrant students because they appear to have a sense of purpose and direction. However, teacher expectations are only one of many forces shaping school-adaptation patterns and do not appear to be as critical as home, community, and peer influences. Like other researchers, Gibson stresses the high aspirations of immigrant students:

> Immigrants, on the whole, have higher educational and occupational aspirations than indigenous groups, majority as well as minority, and are more determined to use education as a strategy for upward social mobility than non-immigrants of comparable class background. Immigrant parents and children assume that education can enhance opportunities to compete for jobs. High expectations and assumptions about the value of schooling appear to have far more impact on the immigrant child's decision to persist in school than either family background or actual school performance. (p. 174)

Finally, this positive pattern of educational achievement is not uniform across all ethnic groups. A major distinction is between Asian immigrants and other groups. The finding that Asian students are more likely to graduate from high school and attend college than either other non-Asian immigrants or native-born students applies not only to the relatively affluent Chinese and Japanese, but also to Filipinos, Koreans, Asian Indians, and Southeast Asians. For example, a study of the close to 20,000 Hmong who settled in Wisconsin between 1975 and 1990 found that, despite the lack of formal parental education or even any written form of native language, Hmong children are performing considerably above the average of native-born students, and most are continuing on in postsecondary education (S. Fass, 1991). Explanations for this pattern range from differences in the educational level that immigrants have attained before arriving in the United States to differences in home environments. One other prominent explanation has been offered by Ogbu (1990). He makes a distinction between immigrant or voluntary minorities and caste-like or involuntary minorities. The category of voluntary minorities includes Asian immigrants, while involuntary minorities include not only blacks and American Indians but also Mexican-Americans. Ogbu places Mexican-Americans in the latter category because Mexican territory in what is now the American

Southwest was conquered by Anglos, and subsequent generations of Mexican-Americans have been treated similarly to blacks and American Indians. Ogbu argues that differences in achievement can be explained by cultural differences that are shaped by a group's own culture and its initial terms of incorporation into American society. Immigrants come to the United States with the expectation of receiving certain economic, political, and social benefits; while they may suffer discrimination, they tend to measure their success or failure by the standards of their homelands, not by those of white Americans. Involuntary minorities, on the other hand, do not hold the same positive expectations about gaining such benefits. These differences, in turn, shape students' responses to the conditions they encounter in schools.

Past studies provide insights into the ways in which immigrants' own cultural conditions and expectations interact with the schooling experiences they encounter upon arriving in the United States. These studies also suggest that it is a fallacy to consider immigrant students as a single group: Relevant comparisons need to be made across immigrants from different ethnic groups, between immigrants and native-born individuals of the same ethnic group, and among immigrants, blacks, and Anglos. Consequently, although the major findings from ethnographic studies of immigrants are largely consistent, generalizing from them to all immigrant students is problematic. These studies are heavily context-dependent and rarely compare schooling conditions and outcomes for immigrant students across different types of communities.

It is also problematic to use such studies for policy purposes. Not only are they idiosyncratic to specific kinds of schools and communities, but they also examine the issue from the perspective of individual students responding to particular cultural and educational milieus. Consideration of immigrant education as a policy issue, on the other hand, requires that we examine it from the perspective of the larger system in which it operates. This broader focus is necessary for understanding how the schooling of immigrant students relates to the overall functioning of the U.S. educational system and for analyzing the resources and constraints that policymakers and educators face in attempting to meet the needs of immigrant students. Two recent reports (National Coalition of Advocates for Students, 1988; Olsen, 1988) by groups working on behalf of immigrant students have detailed their needs and recommended policy directions consistent with meeting those needs. These reports are rare in that they take a policy perspective in assessing the schooling experiences of immigrant youth. But one is limited to California (Olsen, 1988), and both consider immigrant education in isolation, independent of either the functioning of the larger educational system or the other policy demands with which it must compete.

ANALYTICAL PERSPECTIVE AND STUDY METHODS

Research Questions and Conceptual Approach

This study examines immigrant education from a broad policy perspective, explicitly considering it as a political issue in competition for policymakers' attention and scarce public resources, and as one dimension of increasingly overburdened local school systems.[3]   It focuses on four questions:

- What are the social and educational needs of immigrant students?

- What strategies are states, local districts, and individual schools using to educate immigrant students?

- To what extent do current education reform efforts—such as site-based management and more rigorous curricula—complement or hinder districts' and schools' efforts to meet the needs of immigrant students?

- What strategies are likely to be most productive in meeting immigrant students' needs, given the current educational, political, and fiscal climate?

The concentration of immigrant students in a few states and large urban districts suggests a perspective for examining how immigrant education is treated as a policy issue. James Q. Wilson (1989) has argued that, in analyzing the politics of an issue, it is important to con-

---

[3]We chose to examine immigrant education from a policy perspective, concentrating on questions of resource allocation, service delivery, and the political incentives to respond to these students' needs, because so little research has been done from this viewpoint. This emphasis, along with resource and time constraints, meant that we had to sacrifice analyzing the educational needs of immigrant students from the perspective of the students themselves. However, since there are a number of insightful analyses from the imigrant's viewpoint, we felt we could best contribute to an understanding of the issue area by concentrating on the policy-practice side.

sider how diffuse or concentrated its costs and benefits are. Immigration is a policy area where the economic and social benefits generated by newcomers are diffuse and long term. In fact, there is currently a debate among researchers and policymakers about the net effect of immigrants on the U.S. economy. Some analyses (e.g., Simon, 1984; McCarthy and Valdez, 1986) have found that, in the aggregate, immigrants produce a net positive impact, paying more in taxes than they receive in public benefits and helping to maintain a strong industrial and manufacturing base in specific local areas, such as Los Angeles. However, other analysts, such as George Borjas (1990), have pointed to the low educational and skill levels of new immigrants compared to those in earlier waves. These analysts have argued that, while immigrants have not adversely affected the earnings and employment opportunities of native-born workers, the continued influx of the less-skilled may make the United States less competitive internationally and may generate higher welfare and social-service expenditures. These divergent findings can be partially explained by differences in study design—e.g., whether the research focuses on legal and illegal immigration, on all ethnic groups or particular ones, and on one or more levels of government (Stanfield, 1992). In the absence of clear findings, much of the debate on the relative costs and benefits of immigration has tended toward the polemical.

Even if we assume that the most positive findings are correct, however, the benefits of immigration appear diffuse from a national perspective—they tend to be localized in particular industries and geographic areas, and they may materialize only after many years. On the other hand, the costs to the federal government of immigration are also low and diffuse in their impact. Most employed immigrants pay federal income and social security taxes and do not use disproportionate amounts of those services funded by the federal government (e.g., refugees are the only immigrant group that uses welfare to any significant extent). Consequently, there is little incentive for national policymakers to deal with immigrant education. Since both the benefits and the costs are so diffuse, there is little interest-group activity around the issue at the national level, and the constituents of most members of Congress are unaffected by immigration, either positively or negatively. As a result, immigrant education is not on the national policy agenda, and the federal role in immigrant education is limited.

The politics of immigrant education look different at the state and local levels, however. Although the benefits may also be perceived as diffuse and long term at that level, the costs are not. One of the largest costs associated with growing numbers of immigrants is education (McCarthy and Valdez, 1986), the majority of which is borne by states and localities (Shuit and McDonnell, 1992). Therefore, we expected that immigrant education would be primarily a state and local policy issue, with political concern only mobilized in those areas most directly affected. As subsequent chapters will indicate, our assumption about the local level is largely correct. To the extent that the education of immigrants is considered at all as a separate policy issue, it occurs at the local level. But even at this level, the needs of immigrant students are primarily viewed as service-delivery issues that are often addressed on an ad hoc basis in individual schools. As we will argue in Chapter Three, strategies for serving immigrant students are typically not framed as comprehensive or coherent policy, and they are not linked to the broader, systemic needs of urban school districts.

Contrary to our expectations, however, the education of immigrant children is not a definable policy issue at the state level. To the extent that immigrants are considered as a separate category, they are viewed as language-minority students who may also be poor. Chapter Two examines the reasons for a lack of policy attention at the state level.

When we began to examine how policymakers and educators define the policy problems that need to be addressed to assist immigrant children, the types of strategies they select, the resources they can mobilize, and the constraints they face, the fact that immigrant education is a policy area with diffuse benefits and concentrated costs helped explain the patterns we found. Until there is a stronger consensus about the level of societal benefits derived from immigration and whether those benefits should be viewed as national in scope, there is little incentive for national policymakers to assist those states and localities most affected by the costs of educating immigrant children. For the present, the types of services that immigrant students receive are largely shaped by the resources available to the localities where they reside and by the situational imperatives that individual principals and teachers face in attempting to meet these students' needs.

Study Methods

To answer our four research questions, we needed to examine immigrant education in a sample of local districts and schools that reflects the range of communities in which immigrant children now live. We also needed to understand the perceptions and activities of a variety of actors, from the teachers who work directly with these children to the state policymakers responsible for public education. Although an in-depth survey of immigrant students was beyond the scope of this study, we also needed systematic data on their schooling experiences.

Sample. Therefore, we selected a purposive sample of eight school districts and 55 schools in those districts. The districts and the demographic characteristics of their students are summarized in Table 1.4. Six districts—New York, Los Angeles, Chicago, Miami, Houston, and San Francisco—were selected because together they enroll the overwhelming majority of immigrant students nationally. Visalia is a rural district that has experienced a large influx of immigrant students. Although neither the absolute numbers nor the proportions are as great as in the urban areas, large numbers of immigrants are a relatively new phenomenon in rural communities. We included Visalia in the study sample because we assumed that educating immigrant children in areas with traditionally less-diverse populations may pose different kinds of challenges than in more heterogenous cities, and because in such states as California, Florida, and Texas, immigrant students now live in all types of communities and are not concentrated just in urban areas. Similarly, we included Fairfax County because it is a suburban district that has recently experienced a large influx of immigrant students. Although Fairfax is unique in its proximity to Washington, D.C., and the affluence of many of its residents, it is typical of a number of suburban districts that are now enrolling significant numbers of immigrants. For example, in their search for affordable housing, large numbers of immigrants have moved to inner-ring suburbs of San Francisco and Los Angeles, so that these areas now reflect the ethnic diversity of the cities they surround. We assumed that, like the rural communities, these suburban districts may have been accustomed to educating a fairly homogenous student body and would encounter some difficulties in responding to the needs of the newcomers. We also in-

Table 1.4

Study Sample

District	Total Enrollment (1990–1991)	Ethnic Composition (percent)		LEP Students	Recent Immigrants[a]	Major Immigrant Groups
New York City	956,000	Black Hispanic Anglo Asian	38 35 19 8	94,000	70,000	Caribbean Russian Chinese Mexican
Los Angeles	625,461	Hispanic Black Anglo Asian	63 15 14 8	200,500	89,048	Mexican Central American
Chicago	408,714	Black Hispanic Anglo Asian	58 27 12 3	42,000	20,000	Mexican Polish Rumanian South & Southeast Asian Central & South American
Dade County (Miami)	289,727	Hispanic Black Anglo Other	89 5 5 1	40,700	46,994	Nicaraguan Cuban Haitian Columbian Jamaican
Houston	194,512	Hispanic Black Anglo Asian	45 38 14 3	35,027	7,638	Mexican Central American
Fairfax County, VA	131,000	Anglo Asian Black Hispanic	72 12 10 6	6,000	4,801	Southeast Asian Central American Mexican
San Francisco	63,506	Asian Hispanic Black Anglo Other[b]	34 20 19 14 13	18,040	13,317	Chinese Filipino Mexican Central American Southeast Asian
Visalia, CA	21,324	Anglo Hispanic Asian	56 33 8	4,397	1,361	Southeast Asian Mexican

[a]These are students who have lived in the United States for three years or less, and are identified as eligible for federal Emergency Immigrant Education Act (EIEA) funds.

[b]This category includes Arabs, Indo-Chinese, Samoans, and American Indians.

cluded a suburban district in the sample, because current trends suggest that more and more immigrants will move to such communities in search of affordable housing and the jobs no longer available in the central cities.

District and school interviews. In each district, we selected for study those schools with the greatest numbers of immigrant students. However, wherever possible, we also attempted to include schools that have mixed enrollments of native-born and immigrant students and have more than one ethnic group represented in the student body. The sample includes 20 elementary schools, 11 middle schools or junior highs, and 18 high schools. In each school, we conducted either on-site or telephone interviews with principals, teachers, counselors, and bilingual/ESL program coordinators.[4] At the district level, we interviewed school board members, the superintendent or his deputy, the director of the district's bilingual/ESL program, the district curriculum director, and directors of other programs that impact on immigrant students (e.g., student services, compensatory education, and school reform). In each district, we also interviewed representatives of those community groups and social-service agencies serving immigrants. A total of 236 interviews were conducted in the eight school districts.

In addition to questions about district and school-level demographics, governance, program offerings, and policy initiatives, respondents were asked to

- describe the academic and related opportunities available to students—e.g., programs for language-minority students, including how they are assigned, how their progress is monitored and what instructional strategies are used; academic course offerings and how students are assigned to courses; teacher qualifications, including the number who can speak students' native languages

---

[4]In 23 of the schools, on-site interviews were conducted with the following staff: the principal; the bilingual coordinator, if the position existed; the head counselor in high schools; in elementary schools, those teaching kindergarten, third, and sixth grades (and where possible, the appropriate bilingual aides for those teachers); and in high schools, an ESL teacher and the chairs of the mathematics, social studies, and vocational education departments.

In the remaining 32 schools, telephone interviews were conducted with the principal and either the bilingual coordinator or the head counselor.

- describe the types of immigrant students with whom they work—their aspirations and academic performance, attitudes and motivation, linguistic abilities, social skills, and relationships with other students and staff

- assess the major problems faced by immigrant students and the adequacy of the academic and social services available to them

- compare immigrant and native-born students in terms of their needs and school experiences and the types of interactions among them.

The interview data were analyzed in two ways. A site summary was prepared on each district. These summaries, based on the statistical and interview data collected at the district and school levels, included overviews of each district, a description of immigrant education at the district level, and a discussion of school practices as they affect immigrant students. Because the summaries were prepared using a common outline and set of analytical criteria, comparisons could be made across schools within the same district, as well as across the eight districts. In addition, all the interview data were entered into a computerized database that allowed project staff to access responses by district, school, respondent category, or any combination of these. In this way, the data could be aggregated and analyzed more systematically than is typically feasible with qualitative data.

Transcript analysis. To supplement the statistical and interview data collected on districts and schools and to obtain a systematic picture of immigrant students' schooling experiences, we also coded the transcripts of 745 students enrolled in two elementary, two middle, and two high schools in Los Angeles. At the elementary schools, the transcripts of 145 children who were second graders in the 1990-1991 school year and 145 who were fourth graders were randomly sampled and coded. At the middle schools, 150 transcripts of students who were in eighth grade in the 1990-1991 school year were randomly sampled. At the high schools, 152 tenth graders (Class of '93) and 153 eleventh graders (Class of '92) were randomly sampled from ninth grade class lists to ensure that subsequent dropouts were included. Table 1.5 summarizes the demographic characteristics of the six schools from which the transcripts were sampled.

Table 1.5

Characteristics of Los Angeles Schools from Which Student Transcripts Were Sampled (1990-1991)

	Total Enrollment	Percent Recent Immigrants[a]	Ethnicity (percentages)			
			Hispanic	Asian	Black	Anglo
1. Elementary	964	31	61	31	3	5
2. Elementary	1,675	38	80	20	—	—
3. Middle school	1,888	11	62	5	33	—
4. Middle school	1,990	60	63	8	2	27
5. High school	4,327	68	82	16	1	1
6. High school	2,749	24	71	28	—	—

[a]These are students who have lived in the United States for three years or less, and are identified as eligible for federal EIEA funds.

Since we were interested not only in understanding the schooling experiences of immigrant students, but also in comparing them with those of native-born youth, we included both groups in the sampling universe. To ensure that there were sufficient numbers, we over-sampled immigrants by first disaggregating student lists by foreign- and native-born and then randomly sampling from each list. As a result, slightly over half the sample are either recent arrivals who have been in the United States three years or less (31 percent) or more es-tablished immigrants, living in this country for more than three years (23 percent).

Transcripts were coded to obtain the following information on stu-dents:[5]

- background characteristics—gender, ethnicity, immigrant status, eligibility for free or reduced-price lunch (as a proxy for poverty status), whether living with one or both parents or a guardian, mobility, number of absences, suspensions, and retention in grade

---

[5]Approximately 5 percent of the transcripts were independently coded by two differ-ent coders. The reliability analysis on this subsample indicated a 94 percent level of agreement across coders.

- frequency and type of language and achievement testing and the scores on those tests

- types of special services provided—e.g., special education, gifted classes, regular counseling

- type of language instruction—ESL; bilingual; for middle and high school students, whether any academic subjects were taken in students' native language

- types of courses taken, level of courses,[6] and grades for middle and high school students

- teachers' comments about students' overall ability, motivation and effort, concentration, social behavior, and classroom behavior for elementary students.[7]

Because of resource limitations, we could only conduct a transcript analysis on one school district. We chose Los Angeles, because it is the district most affected by immigrants. As the discussion in Chapter Three indicates, language instruction and curricular offerings for immigrant and other language-minority students differ from district to district. Consequently, the transcript analysis reported in

---

[6]The academic level of each course was coded in one of seven categories: *remedial*—instruction aimed at remediating basic skill deficiencies; *regular/basic*—academic material presented in a manner suitable for students who will end their formal schooling with high school, emphasizing exposure and basic competencies; *applied/vocational*—content focused on students' possible vocational objectives, emphasizing applications in the work setting; *heterogeneous*—material appropriate for students with a variety of abilities and educational objectives; *college-preparatory*—material that gives students academic skills and breadth of exposure sufficient to prepare them for college-level work; *honors*—college-preparatory content, but enriched or accelerated; *advanced*—material that prepares students for advanced placement (AP) examinations.

Three other pieces of information were coded for each course: whether the course was taught as a bilingual, ESL, or sheltered class; when the course was taken; and the grade a student received.

The coding of this information was based on in-depth interviews with school staff, a review of course handbooks and other materials, and follow-up telephone inquiries, as needed for clarification.

The procedures and coding categories used for the transcript analysis were developed as part of earlier research on the design of curriculum indicators. See McDonnell et al. (1990).

[7]Although grades are not given at this level, teachers do rate students' achievement and effort in academic subjects and their classroom behavior as either *satisfactory* or *unsatisfactory*. These teacher judgments were also coded.

that chapter is only generalizable to schools in Los Angeles with high proportions of immigrant students. Nevertheless, it does present a portrait of how well immigrant students in the "New Ellis Island" are faring.

State-level interviews. A final data source is interviews conducted with state policymakers in California, Florida, Illinois, New York, Texas, and Virginia. Respondents included state legislators and their staffs, governors' education aides, the leadership of the states' departments of education, administrators of bilingual and federal immigrant programs, and interest-group representatives. Thirty-eight interviews were conducted across the six states.

Respondents were asked about how state policymakers assess the importance of immigrant education in comparison with other education issues, how they define the problems that need to be addressed in the schooling of immigrant youth, the operations and adequacy of state programs to serve immigrant students, the adequacy of federal programs, any perceived gaps in the services available to immigrant students, and the major issues facing the state with regard to the education of immigrant students.

ORGANIZATION OF THE REPORT

Although the federal role in immigrant education was not a specific focus of our study, it sets a legal and policy context for state and local activities. Therefore, the first part of Chapter Two presents a brief summary of federal policies that directly affect immigrant students; the remainder of the chapter draws on the state-level interviews in analyzing the state role in immigrant education. Findings based on the district- and school-level data are presented in Chapters Three and Four. In Chapter Five, we argue that, although immigrant students have unmet educational needs unique to their newcomer status, the greatest barrier to quality education for them is the same as it is for all students in urban school districts. Simply put, those districts lack the basic institutional capacity to meet the educational and social needs of their students. Consequently, we recommend several strategies specific to improving educational outcomes for immigrant students, but then stress the more fundamental changes that will be necessary to strengthen the entire system responsible for educating students in large city schools.

Chapter Two

FEDERAL AND STATE ROLES IN IMMIGRANT EDUCATION

A LIMITED FEDERAL PRESENCE

The federal government plays a narrowly circumscribed role in the schooling of immigrant students, similar to its function in elementary and secondary education generally. At a programmatic level, it acts as a junior partner, funding several categorical programs that supplement the costs borne by states and local districts. But it also plays another, more substantial, role, because federal judicial decisions create frameworks that define the legal rights of various student groups. For immigrant students, the *Lau* remedies are the most relevant. These are based on the 1974 Supreme Court decision, which ruled that, under Title VI of the Civil Rights Act, LEP students are entitled to special assistance to allow them to participate equally in school programs.

The one federal program specifically targeted to immigrant students, the Emergency Immigrant Education Act (EIEA), is small, with total appropriations of $30 million a year.[1] To qualify for EIEA funding, a school district must have at least 500 immigrant students, or these

---

[1]Until FY 1989, the federal government also funded the Transition Program for Refugee Children (TPRC). In its last year, the program was funded at $15 million to serve 74,000 refugee children. Although the amount available per eligible student (about $200) was considerably higher than for EIEA, the per capita funding had decreased from about $650 per student in the program's early years.

students must represent at least 3 percent of its total enrollment.[2] Students can only be counted for EIEA funding if they have been in U.S. schools for three years or less.[3] In FY 1990, the total amount of EIEA funds available per student was $42, down from $86 per student six years earlier. The decrease resulted because appropriations have remained stable, while the number of eligible students has increased by 73 percent.

Despite the relatively small amount of EIEA funding generated per student, districts welcome the money because they have wide latitude in how it can be spent. They may use it for personnel expenses incurred in remedial instructional programs, the training of staff to work with immigrant students, instructional materials for English language and bilingual programs, and the requisition of classroom space. School districts can use the funds to benefit any or all of their students, as long as the services are related to the educational needs of EIEA-eligible immigrants. In 1991, the General Accounting Office (GAO) reported that about 80 percent of EIEA funds was used to support academic instructional programs. The remaining 20 percent was used for such purposes as student testing and counseling, parental involvement activities, and administrative services (GAO, 1991).

A second federal program directly relevant to immigrant students is Title VII of the Elementary and Secondary Education Act (ESEA), which funds instructional programs for LEP students, whether they are immigrants or native born. The bulk of the funds ($115.8 million in FY 1990) is awarded to school districts in the form of discretionary project grants of three years' duration. With project funding, district staff design and implement instructional programs for language-minority students. The majority (64 percent of the 800 funded in FY 1990) are designed as transitional bilingual programs, with instruc-

---

[2]The GAO estimated that during the 1989–1990 school year, there were 700,000 immigrants who met EIEA eligibility criteria. However, only 564,000 (85 percent) were enrolled in the 529 districts that received EIEA funds. The remaining immigrant youth were dispersed among an estimated 4000 school districts that did not receive EIEA funding (GAO, 1991).

[3]As another indication of the concentration of immigrant students, in FY 1990, California received 45 percent of the available EIEA funds based on its numbers of eligible students. Together, California, Florida, Illinois, New York, and Texas received 78 percent of the total EIEA funding.

tion in both a student's native language and English, and are intended to achieve student proficiency in English. A few projects (2 percent) are designed as developmental bilingual programs to help LEP students attain competence in their native languages and in English. About 20 percent of the projects support structured English-language instruction for LEP students, and the remaining projects focus on special purposes, such as instruction for LEP students in preschool, special education, gifted and talented programs, and English literacy instruction for parents. About 290,000 of the 1.9 million LEP students nationwide were served in Title VII projects during FY 1990 (U.S. Department of Education, 1991). The remaining Title VII funds ($41 million in FY 1990) are used for technical assistance and staff development, data collection, and evaluation. The GAO estimates that in 1990, about 19 to 31 percent of recent immigrants in districts with EIEA funds were receiving instructional services from a Title VII project (GAO, 1991).

Although programs funded by Title VII deliver instructional services to immigrant and other language-minority students, they neither serve all such students nor are they a stable source of program funding. From its inception in 1968, Title VII was meant to stimulate innovative programs that would eventually be supported by state and local funds. In addition, local districts are under no obligation to apply for such funds. Consequently, whether a given student receives Title VII services depends on whether the district in which he or she is enrolled is interested in mounting a program and on that district's ability to compete successfully for funding.

In addition to services funded by EIEA and Title VII, immigrant students may receive federally funded services under the Chapter 1 programs for educationally disadvantaged and migrant children.[4] The GAO estimates that, in the 1989–1990 school year, between 50 and 66 percent of the recent immigrants in districts receiving EIEA funds also received Chapter 1 services for educationally disadvantaged children, and between 15 and 24 percent received migrant education services (GAO, 1991).

---

[4]Chapter 1 is the largest federal elementary and secondary education program, with appropriations of $5.2 billion in FY 1990. It funds supplemental remedial instruction and is intended to serve educationally disadvantaged students in school districts with relatively high concentrations of children from low-income families.

The federal initiative that has had the greatest impact on the services available to immigrant students is not a programmatic one authorized through legislation, but rather the result of litigation. In a 1974 decision, *Lau v. Nichols*, the U.S. Supreme Court overturned the decision of a federal district court in a class action suit brought four years earlier on behalf of Chinese students against the San Francisco Unified School District. The plaintiffs argued that no programs were available to meet the students' specific linguistic needs and that, as a result, they suffered educationally because they could not benefit from instruction in English. The Court, in an opinion authored by Justice Douglas, ruled that

> There is no equality of treatment merely by providing students with the same facilities, textbooks, teachers, and curriculum; for students who do not understand English are effectively foreclosed from any meaningful education. (414 U.S. 563)

Three aspects of the decision and its aftermath are important. First, although the plaintiffs argued on the basis of both their constitutional rights under the equal protection clause of the Fourteenth Amendment and Title VI of the 1964 Civil Rights Act, the Court avoided the constitutional issue altogether and used Title VI as the basis for its decision. In other words, the ruling invoked no constitutional guarantees for language-minority students (Hakuta, 1986; Crawford, 1991). Second, by the time the case had reached the Supreme Court, the plaintiffs had dropped their earlier demand for bilingual education. Consequently, the Court acted consistently with previous decisions that specific educational remedies be left to local school boards and ruled that

> No specific remedy is urged upon us. Teaching English to the students of Chinese ancestry who do not speak the language is one choice. Giving instructions to this group in Chinese is another. There may be others. Petitioners ask only that the Board of Education be directed to apply its expertise to the problem and rectify the situation.[5]

---

[5]In a consent decree, the San Francisco Board of Education agreed to provide a bilingual-bicultural program for the Chinese, Filipino, and Spanish-speaking students who constitute over 80 percent of the LEP students in the district. For the remaining groups, ESL instruction was offered.

The discretion that the Court permitted local districts in fashioning a remedy was subsequently narrowed by a set of policy guidelines promulgated by the U.S. Office of Education. Developed by a task force comprising Office of Civil Rights (OCR) staff and outside bilingual education experts, what became known as the *Lau* remedies outlined how districts should identify and evaluate children with limited English skills, what instructional strategies are appropriate for them, the criteria for mainstreaming LEP students, and what professional standards teachers should meet. Most importantly, the remedies went beyond the *Lau* decision in requiring that, when a student's rights had been violated, districts must provide bilingual instruction for students who speak little or no English. "English as a second language is a necessary component" of bilingual instruction, the guidelines stated, but "since an ESL program does not consider the affective nor cognitive development of the students . . . an ESL program [by itself] is *not* appropriate" (as cited in Crawford, 1991, p. 37). In most cases, compensatory instruction in English alone was considered, according to the guidelines, to be permissible for secondary students. Although the *Lau* remedies lacked the force of federal regulations, they were used as the basis for OCR enforcement actions and as a condition of funding for districts applying for Title VII support.

A third notable aspect of *Lau* and the federal role in educating language-minority children has been the intense level of controversy surrounding it—far greater than would be predicted by either the modest funding level of Title VII or a Supreme Court decision that received a one-sentence mention in the *New York Times* when it was first rendered (Hakuta, 1986; Crawford, 1991). Reasons for the continuing high levels of controversy are severalfold, but most can be traced to the unresolved conflict between bilingual education as a means of smoothing children's transition into English language instruction or as a vehicle for the maintenance of their native language and culture. This ambivalence and the resulting tension can be traced to the passage of Title VII in 1968 when, to get the legislation enacted, its supporters kept both the definition of bilingual education and the purpose of the Act intentionally vague (Ravitch, 1983). As Hakuta (1986, p. 226) notes, bilingual education "carries with it the burden of a societal symbol." As such, it has been the focal point of debates over how assimilationist the schools should be; whether additional public resources should be provided for a specific group of students and their teachers, the majority of whom are members of a single ethnic group; and, depending on the goals of bilingual education, what the most appropriate and effective instructional strategies are. Over the past 25 years, these questions have been addressed not as pedagogical issues, but as highly emotional, political ones, with the answers dependent on which ideological position is ascendant at any given time.

AN INVISIBLE POLICY ISSUE FOR STATES

The most notable characteristic of immigrant education policy at the state level is its total absence, aside from programs for LEP students. Across the six states we studied, there are no policies specifically targeted to students on the basis of their immigrant status. Rather, state policy focuses on students with limited English-language skills, whether they be immigrants or native born. Beyond this overarching feature, state policy affecting immigrant students is typical of other areas of elementary and secondary education in that it varies considerably from state to state, while also exhibiting important commonalities.

Four common factors characterize immigrant education across the six states. First, it is not a very visible issue. As one state senator in Illinois noted, "immigrant education is an issue there with dozens of others, but it's not at the top." Policymakers acknowledge immigrant education as important, but either view it as subsumed under other issues, such as dropout prevention, or rank it on the state policy agenda considerably below such issues as school finance reform or coping with budgetary pressures. Second, immigrant education policy is essentially English-language acquisition policy. Every state policymaker we interviewed, regardless of role, position, or political ideology, equated the two. Third, to the extent that immigrant education policy is language acquisition policy, it is the product of both judicial and legislative actions. Those pressing for improved instruction for language-minority students have used the federal courts to force greater state effort in this area. In a majority of states with large immigrant populations, judicial decisions have played a key role in shaping the state program, usually by requiring that the state guarantee a level of services to eligible students and monitor the type and quality of instruction provided by local districts. Acting in response to constituent pressure and judicial mandates, the legislatures in all six states have dealt with the issue through policies that typically require local districts to provide instructional services to LEP students and provide a modest level of state support. Finally, a major similarity across the six states is that, in each state, policy mechanisms do make a difference. The mandates and incentives that constitute state policy for LEP students create frameworks that significantly shape the kinds of services those students receive in local districts.

Major differences across the six states are twofold. First, the politics of bilingual education, and hence immigrant education, vary considerably from state to state. In Illinois and New York, the state bilingual program is well established, viewed as another categorical program to meet the needs of a particular constituency, and insulated from political assaults. Although the programs may be somewhat less well institutionalized, the legislative politics of bilingual education in Florida and Texas are similar to those in Illinois and New York, with the program largely viewed as assistance to one area of the state. In California, on the other hand, bilingual education has been a continuing source of controversy: The state legislature was unable to override a gubernatorial veto, thus preventing reauthorization of the state program after its mandated sunset in 1986. Finally, Virginia has traditionally considered the education of LEP and immigrant students to be a local problem, and only recently have state policymakers begun to deal with the issue. The second difference is the extent to which the policy responses of the six states vary. At one end of the continuum is Virginia, where legislators have appropriated a small amount of state funds ($1.7 million in the 1990 biennium) to be allocated to local school districts serving LEP students. At the other end is Illinois, where, as the result of state program mandates, large numbers of LEP students have access to a college-preparatory curriculum in their native language. As we will see in this chapter and the next, the extent to which instruction for LEP students varies across states largely depends on the nature of the LEP population and the availability of qualified teachers. Nevertheless, the strength of state mandates and the funding levels also help account for differences.

The remainder of this chapter examines these similarities and differences by first focusing on how the issue of immigrant education is viewed in the state policy arena and on how the politics of the issue have shaped state policy responses. The state policy frameworks for each of the six states are then compared.

Immigrant Education as the Politics of Bilingual Education

Defining the Problem. State-level respondents were asked, "when policymakers consider schooling for immigrant children, what do they see as the major problems that need to be addressed?" With few exceptions, the problem of immigrant education is viewed by state policymakers as the need for newcomers to learn English. For example, one Hispanic legislator in Texas noted, "this is a black and white issue—it's bilingual education. [Policymakers] see the language barrier as the hardest obstacle to overcome for recent immigrants." Likewise, the governor's education aide in New York noted that, "for most policymakers, immigrant education is about helping students learn English." Even state-level advocacy groups for immigrants, such as the California Rural Legal Assistance Foundation, define the problem similarly: "we view the needs of immigrant students similar to those of LEPs. Immigrant is a substitute for LEP."

The extent to which the issue is viewed as the need to acquire English-language proficiency, even when that may not be the main problem facing an immigrant student, was noted by a state education department official in New York:

> When you ask policymakers about immigrants, they will respond in terms of those who are LEP. Yet we have English-speaking immigrants from the West Indies who have special needs, and their needs are becoming evident in New York City and Westchester. These students have minimal educational backgrounds; their spoken English is different from either American or standard English; and they come from a very different cultural environment. The state has no policy yet about whether services should be required for this English-speaking group of immigrants, but we are aware of them from the EIEA counts.[6]

---

[6]In FY 1990, about 14 percent of New York students who had been in the United States for three years or less were from English-speaking countries.

A few respondents in each state, however, saw the problems facing immigrant students in a broader context. For example, a number of respondents in California mentioned that there was a need to provide more and better training for adult immigrants. In their view, that training includes the opportunity to gain what has been called "an employability level of English proficiency." But it also includes vocational training that would allow for upward occupational mobility. Expanded educational opportunities for adult immigrants are also viewed as a way to assist immigrant children by improving the economic status of their families and giving parents skills that will enable them to help their children do well in school. There was also a sense among respondents who mentioned the need for adult education that such services commanded widespread political support and are a way to help immigrants, while avoiding the controversy surrounding bilingual education.

In discussing the English-language acquisition needs of immigrant students, some respondents mentioned related needs not currently being met. For example, California respondents talked about the school facilities shortages that have resulted in overcrowded schools and long-distance busing in some districts, most notably Los Angeles. A related problem mentioned with some frequency is the shortage of teachers qualified to teach LEP students. A California state department of education task force reported that in 1989 the state had a shortage of 11,710 bilingual teachers. The absolute numbers are greatest for Spanish: Only half of the over 600,000 Spanish-speaking children in California are taught by a teacher who speaks Spanish, with the state estimating that the shortage of Spanish bilingual teachers is close to 8,000 (Berman et al., 1992; California SDE Task Force, 1990). But the need is also high in other languages, such as Vietnamese, for which 716 teachers are needed, with only 46 currently available. Similarly, the state education department in New York reported in 1990 that 32 percent of the ESL teachers in the state and 48 percent of the bilingual teachers lacked the appropriate certification (New York State Education Department, 1990).

Explanations for why immigrant and bilingual education have become synonymous focused on the fact that, even in states with large immigrant populations, most legislators do not have immigrants living in their districts, because immigrants tend to concentrate in only a few areas of the state. Legislators representing heavily immigrant districts spoke of colleagues' misconceptions about bilingual education—for example, that nothing was ever taught or learned in English. Even in California, where immigrants now live throughout most of the state, one legislative staffer estimated that "fewer than a quarter of the members of the senate have a sense of the problems faced by immigrants—not just in education, but in health and other areas . . . they're not in schools very often."

The State Politics of Bilingual Education. The linking of immigrant education with bilingual education has meant, on the one hand, that there is a relatively stable source of state funding to assist newcomers. But it has also meant that schooling conditions for immigrant students are inextricably linked to the state politics of bilingual education. In Illinois and New York, those politics have been routinized. Bilingual education is viewed as one of a number of categorical programs in both states. Although one Hispanic legislator in New York characterized attempts to fund the state bilingual program as "like milking a reluctant cow," the program is funded through the state aid formula with the supplement having increased from 0.05 of per capita student funding (ADA) in 1981 to the current 0.15 ADA. In Illinois, one legislative leader in education characterized the bilingual program as now safe from attempts either to reduce funding or to abolish the program. His Hispanic colleague agreed, noting:

> There has been an increase in the immigrant population outside Chicago in the collar counties. This has increased political support because elected officials are being forced to be responsive as larger numbers of immigrants move into their areas. That's why we no longer have to fear the elimination of bilingual funding, and can now begin to concentrate on the quality of programs. . . .

> You no longer hear people talking about whether or not they are going to cut us. This is allowing us in the Hispanic community to shed bilingual education as a sacred cow. We could see deficiencies in bilingual education in the past, but we were afraid to air our dirty laundry. Now we can criticize the quality without fear of opening up the program for attack, and having the baby thrown out with the bath water.

Even though it is now viewed as a categorical program serving a particular constituency, bilingual-education advocates in Illinois must still moderate their demands. One of the legislative committee chairs characterized the dilemma in this way:

> For the groups interested in bilingual education, there's a tight line between advocacy and killing the golden goose. If these groups are too loud, they may become a target of those trying to kill the program.

Still, as a state department of education official noted,

> over the years, the bilingual program has had its ups and downs, and has been the subject of many legislative debates. It has been perceived as a 'Chicago program,' and as a 'Hispanic program.' But the program has never been cut.[7]

Additionally, in both New York and Illinois, bilingual supporters have been able to block attempts to place English Only initiatives[8] on the state policy agenda.

The extent to which immigrant and bilingual education has been defined as constituency politics in Illinois is illustrated by the only state-level program specifically for immigrants that we found in any of the six states. In Chicago, an alternative school, the Senn Southeast Asian Center, was begun in 1990. Over the first year of the program, about 70 students were served, 30 of whom were newcomers and 40 were refugees who had been in the United States for

---

[7]Unlike funding for bilingual education in Florida, New York, and Texas, where it is allocated through a proportional supplement to the state funding formula, Illinois funds its program through an excess-cost reimbursement system. As the result of a two-year state income surcharge imposed in 1989, state support for education increased, with funding for the bilingual program increasing from $18.9 million to $48.3 million. Consequently, the state reimbursed local districts about 89 percent of their costs in 1990 and about 75 percent in 1991.

[8]Legislation has now been passed in 17 states to make English the official state language through either constitutional amendments or special statutes. Some of these laws are largely symbolic, while others, such as California's Proposition 63, are stronger, because they give individuals the right to sue to enforce the law. The impetus behind the English Only movement is a coalition of interest groups ranging from the 240,000-member U.S. English to the American Grange, the American Legion, and the Polish-American Congress (McGroarty, 1992).

two to five years and had dropped out of school. The program was established by the Governor's Office for Asian-American Affairs and the State Board of Education after Asian community groups lobbied the governor on behalf of Southeast Asian students who entered the United States in their late teens with little formal schooling and were at high risk of dropping out. The program is funded by state truancy, vocational education, adult education, bilingual, and job training funds. The governor's staff portrays the Southeast Asian Center as evidence of the importance of immigrant education at the state level, and the state department of education sees it as a model of interprogram coordination. Yet there are no plans to expand the program or to establish additional ones. Just as bilingual education is viewed as a measure of political influence in the Hispanic community, as well as meeting a critical educational need, the Southeast Asian Center represents both political responsiveness to a growing constituency and an effort to deal with the problem of Asian dropouts.

The politics of bilingual education are somewhat less stable in Florida and Texas. An English Only initiative was passed by Florida voters, but its effect on schools has been minimal, as long as LEP programs can demonstrate that they prepare students for eventual instruction in English. The requirements under which local districts now operate as the result of a recent consent decree (described below) give the option of providing basic subject-area instruction in either a student's home language or in an ESL program. Either method qualifies for an additional 0.6 (ADA) in per-pupil state support for each LEP student. Although the state has provided additional support for LEP students since 1973, it was not until 1990 that the legislature first enacted a law requiring that statewide educational standards for language minorities be established. Study respondents reported that state policymakers gave districts the option of either bilingual or ESL programs as a way of accommodating both sides in a continuing controversy between those advocating bilingual and bicultural education and those insisting on a rapid transition to instruction solely in English.

As in Illinois and New York, attempts to pass an English Only initiative were effectively stopped in Texas, and like New York and Florida, the state funds its bilingual program through the state aid formula (at 0.1 additional ADA). At the same time, Hispanic legislators and their colleagues representing the border areas and the large cities have been forced to retreat from pro-immigrant positions. According to these respondents, if they push immigrant and bilingual issues too strongly, they lose support from their other constituents.

The politics of bilingual education have been the most rancorous in California. The fight against bilingual education was led by conservative Republican members of the Assembly who found an ally in the former governor, George Deukmejian. The opponents of bilingual education maintained that it was too prescriptive and there was no evidence that the program worked. As one example of the prescriptiveness of the program, opponents pointed to the requirement that one-third of each bilingual classroom comprise native English speakers. When the child of one legislator leading the fight against bilingual education was placed in such a class, opponents had a visible rallying point. The fight was acrimonious, with the opponents charging that "the major agenda of the state bilingual program is the Hispanic agenda: to promote Spanish as an equal culture in the state, just like in Quebec." In response, groups advocating bilingual education charged that the opponents were "mean-spirited and xenophobic" and were using the issue merely for political gain. With the issue framed in this way, the strengths and weaknesses of the state program were never debated in a considered manner. Three attempts to reauthorize the bilingual program were vetoed by the governor; currently, state funding for LEP students is contained in a broader compensatory education program, with only the intent of the former legislation (but not its specific requirements) in place.[9]

In Virginia, immigrant students have traditionally lived only in the northern part of the state surrounding Washington, D.C., and in the tidewater region. Consequently, state policymakers were able to define the issue as a local problem. However, as immigrants have begun to locate in other areas of the state, the issue has moved to the

---

[9]Recently, the political debate in California has focused more directly on immigrants and their claim to public services and less on the issue of bilingual education. However, this debate is likely to be no less divisive. As the state's fiscal problems have grown, the current governor, Pete Wilson, has argued that immigrants are among the "tax receivers" who are resettling in California to take advantage of the state's high level of public assistance benefits. The inference that immigrants are a net drain on the state mirrors the results of a 1991 *Los Angeles Times* poll, which found that more than two-thirds of those surveyed considered immigrants to be more of a burden than a benefit to the state (Stanfield, 1992).

state-level agenda. The governor, Douglas Wilder, officially identified immigrant education as an area of concern in his Commission
on Disparity, an initiative to foster equal educational opportunity.
The state also now recognizes LEP students as a category of at-risk
students and is developing a statewide education improvement plan
for LEP students. The expectation is that the original $1.7 million
appropriated in 1990 will be increased this year, with more state
support available for ESL programs.

The state politics of immigrant education are indeed the politics of
bilingual education, with all the emotional baggage that the term has
come to imply. Immigrant and bilingual education are synonymous
not just because politicians have viewed them as one and the same,
but also because the most visible advocates for immigrants are
among the strongest proponents of bilingual programs. With the
rare exception of such groups as California Tomorrow, which focuses
specifically on immigrant children, those interest groups that seek to
improve schooling for immigrants have bilingual education at the
centerpiece of their agenda. The result for immigrants is that they
are assured some critical services, but they can also become pawns
in a political game that may have little to do with the effectiveness of
a particular instructional strategy. However, as the examples of
Illinois and New York illustrate, acrimonious debate may diminish
over time, and questions of program implementation and effectiveness can then move to the forefront.

The Role of the Courts. For a variety of reasons, bilingual education
policy does not lend itself to the majoritarian politics that
characterize state legislatures. Because bilingual education benefits
only a minority of students, taps strongly held beliefs about cultural
identity, and lacks a consensus about goals, even sympathetic
legislators have often found it difficult to build adequate support to
sustain a major program effort. Consequently, bilingual advocates
have turned to the federal courts as the political institution designed
to protect minority rights. The state bilingual programs in California,
Florida, Illinois, and Texas have all been affected by judicial decisions regulating the level and quality of services available to LEP stu-

dents.[10] In this subsection, we summarize three judicial actions that have been critical in shaping the services available to immigrant and LEP students. These decisions are examples of how the federal constitutional framework has provided a basis for requiring state and local action.[11]

The first, *Plyler v. Doe* (102 S. Ct. 2382), is the case most directly relevant to immigrant children. In *Plyler*, the U.S. Supreme Court ruled in 1982 that the states had a responsibility to educate the children of undocumented immigrants and held for the first time that the equal protection clause of the fourteenth amendment extends to anyone, "whether citizens or strangers," who resides within the boundaries of a state, regardless of immigration status (Hull, 1983). Texas had included in its education code a provision that allowed local school districts to charge undocumented children tuition or to prohibit them from attending school. By the mid-1970s, the majority of the state's school districts were refusing to enroll undocumented children, and some districts, such as Houston and Tyler, were charging tuition of $1000 or more, effectively barring poor, immigrant children from school. Sixteen separate court cases were consolidated for trial in the Southern District of Texas. The district court and the Fifth Circuit Court of Appeals found the policy to be unconstitutional and ordered that the students be enrolled in school.

Texas appealed the case to the Supreme Court. The state argued that it was the "height of hypocrisy" for Congress not to bear the costs of educating undocumented children who were in the United States because the federal government was unable or unwilling to enforce its immigration laws. Sixty different groups representing a wide variety of views filed amicus briefs urging the Court to uphold or invalidate the Texas law. Very few cases have elicited such a response or prompted such divisiveness as *Plyler*. This divisiveness was further reflected in the five to four vote of the Court and in the substance of the majority and dissenting opinions (Hull, 1983). Writing for the majority, Justice Brennan concluded that undocumented aliens do

---

[10]Advocates for LEP students have also filed successful lawsuits in New York City, but those decisions affect services only to students in the city and not the state-level program.

[11]For a more general discussion of litigation with regard to the education of language minority students, see August and Garcia (1988).

not constitute a "suspect class" for which heightened judicial solicitude is appropriate. Unlike racial minorities, who are penalized for characteristics over which they have no control, undocumented immigrants are penalized for voluntary conduct that is deliberately unlawful. However, Brennan suggested that, at least in some circumstances, undocumented immigrants constitute a "sensitive" class. As a result of lax enforcement of immigration laws, there exists a "shadow population" of illegal immigrants. According to Brennan,

> This situation raises the specter of a permanent caste of undocumented resident aliens, encouraged by some to remain here as a source of cheap labor, but nevertheless denied the benefits that our society makes available to citizens and lawful residents.

Brennan portrayed undocumented children as a particularly sensitive class. Although a state might withhold benefits from those whose presence in the United States is the result of their own unlawful conduct, he argued, such logic is considerably weakened when the targets are the minor children of undocumented immigrants. To punish those children violates the "basic concept of our system that legal burdens should bear some relationship to individual responsibility or wrongdoing." In the majority opinion, Brennan also addressed a number of the defendants' arguments, including that prohibiting undocumented children from attending school free of charge preserved the state's limited resources for its lawful residents. Justice Brennan wrote that a concern for the preservation of resources could not justify singling out a discrete class of children for discrimination and that evidence presented in the district court demonstrated that immigrants are a net gain to the public treasury. Similarly, Brennan dismissed the argument that providing a free public education would serve as a magnet for further immigration, noting that few families emigrated for educational rather than employment reasons.

The main thrust of the dissenting opinion, written by Chief Justice Burger, was that, in seeking to solve a social problem, the Court majority was formulating new policy, rather than interpreting law. The Court, according to this argument, should not be compensating for the lack of "effective leadership" in Congress.

For immigrant children, *Plyler* was significant in that it established their right to free public schooling, and although the entitlement to public benefits was limited to education, the case also extended the right of equal protection to undocumented immigrants, whether adults or children.

The second and third cases focus more specifically on bilingual education. *Gomez v. Illinois State Board of Education* (811 F.2d 1030) was a 1985 class-action suit filed against the state of Illinois by the Mexican American Legal Defense and Education Fund (MALDEF). The plaintiffs argued that the state was not meeting its obligations under the federal Equal Educational Opportunities Act (EEOA), because some local districts had not tested students for English proficiency and were not providing bilingual instruction, despite a state law mandating such services. The state took the position that it promulgated a set of regulations, but left it to the discretion of local districts to implement those requirements. The plaintiffs lost in district court, but prevailed in the Seventh Circuit. The decision stated that

> State agencies cannot in the guise of deferring to local conditions, completely delegate in practice their obligations under the EEOA; otherwise, the term "educational agency" no longer includes those at the state level.

The case was remanded to the district court, and MALDEF entered into a settlement with the state. The state has agreed to modify its regulations, provide for greater enforcement of local district activities, and implement standard criteria across the state to assess students. The assessment criteria are an example of where local discretion permitted a wide variation in practice. Before the *Gomez* case, state regulations required that a student be considered LEP (and therefore, entitled to services) if he or she fell below the average proficiency of English-speaking students in the same age group. Within that definition, the state allowed districts to set the entry and exit criteria for program services, and some set them low. As a result of the consent decree, the state will now establish uniform and multiple criteria. A standardized test with a specific cutoff point will be used, so students can be compared to national norms. Districts will also be required to assess how students perform on the district's own criterion reference test, and to examine the student's educational history.

The *Gomez* case is an example of how advocacy groups have been able to ensure a more uniform level of services for LEP students through judicial decisions that require state governments to strengthen enforcement activities, but also provide additional leverage that can be brought to bear in the face of potential political opposition. In fact, for allies of bilingual education within state departments of education, relevant judicial decisions become both a rationale and a resource for taking a more activist stance in program management. For example, after the sunset of the bilingual program in California, the Superintendent of Public Instruction, Bill Honig, and the staff of the state office of bilingual education used the rulings in the *Gomez* case and in another case, *Castaneda v. Pickard,*[12] to issue an advisory to local districts that maintained the intent of the former program, despite the absence of a strong state framework. The standards derived from these cases now constitute the basis on which the California state department of education monitors local districts.

The final judicial action, exemplifying the role of the courts in setting state policy for LEP students, is the consent decree reached in 1990 between the state of Florida and a coalition of advocacy groups led by Multicultural Education, Training, and Advocacy, Inc. (META).[13] The coalition charged that the state was failing to provide an adequate education for language-minority students in many parts of the state and pressed for state standards to ensure equal educational opportunities for LEP students in each of the state's 67 school districts.

---

[12]*Castaneda v. Pickard* (648 F.2d 989) is a 1981 case decided in the Fifth Circuit. It found that the EEOA imposes on educational agencies a duty to take appropriate action to remedy the language barriers of students. In deciding whether a particular district's approach to language remediation is appropriate, the court must ascertain that the district is pursuing a program informed by an educational theory recognized as sound by experts, whether or not the school system's practices are reasonably calculated to implement that theory effectively, and whether that program is actually overcoming the language barriers faced by students. *Castaneda* also addresses the need for qualified personnel in such programs and the monitoring of student progress.

[13]Also pressing the lawsuit were the League of United Latin American Citizens (LULAC), the Florida State Conference of the National Association for the Advancement of Colored People (NAACP), the Haitian Refugee Center, the Haitian Educators Association, the Spanish-American League Against Discrimination, the Central Florida Farmworkers Association, the American Hispanic Educators Association of Dade, Aspira, and several Hispanic and Haitian parents and students.

The Commissioner of Education, Betty Castor, agreed to enter into negotiations with the plaintiffs after she determined that smaller school districts needed more state direction in dealing with LEP students (Schmidt, 1990). After a year of negotiations, a consent order was issued by the federal district court, thus giving the court the power to enforce what has become known as the META agreement.

Although local districts have an option under the agreement to provide either native-language instruction in basic subjects or ESL instruction, the state now has standards governing the qualifications of teachers working in those programs and the assessment and placement of students. Advocacy groups characterized the META agreement as "the most extensive statewide expansion of services for language-minority students to be approved anywhere in the country in the past ten years" (Schmidt, 1990).

As these three cases illustrate, advocates on behalf of immigrant and LEP students have been able to press for expanded and improved services through the courts. A series of federal judicial decisions, beginning with *Lau*, has provided a basis for requiring greater state attention to language-minority students. These decisions have acted as a counterpoise to moves against bilingual education in the legislative arena and as a resource for political allies wishing to institutionalize a substantial state program.

State Policy Instruments and Program Frameworks

Given the significant influence of federal regulation and judicial decisions on state programs, it is not surprising that mandates dominate as the underlying policy instrument in state programs for LEP students. With the exception of Virginia, all the states in our study sample regulate which students are served and the services they should receive. These mandates constitute a minimum standard of service that districts must meet. The states also provide modest inducements that local districts can use in meeting those mandates, but three of the six states provide less than $150 per student,[14] with

---

[14]Because the funds targeted for bilingual programs in California prior to the sunset of the state program have now been consolidated into the Economic Impact Aid (EIA) block grant, there is no guarantee that the $100 million generated by LEP students is

the most generous providing about $1500.[15] Each of the states also provides some capacity-building assistance to local districts, with Illinois and New York providing the most comprehensive and sustained assistance.

As Table 2.1 indicates, Illinois, New York, and Texas have the most specific service requirements for LEP students. The major difference among these states is the basis on which they determine that a district must offer a bilingual program, with Illinois using the stricter standard—20 students speaking the same language in the same school building or attendance center—and New York and Texas using students per grade level as the criterion. New York only requires that those districts receiving state funds meet its mandates, but districts refusing these funds are smaller ones and enroll less than 10 percent of the state's students.

Illinois has a two-tiered approach to service mandates for language minority students. During the Reagan administration, when the federal government largely abandoned its regulatory role under *Lau*, the Illinois State Board of Education (SBE) considered weakening its mandates and leaving service decisions to local districts. The SBE was leaning toward local determination, but the Hispanic community in Chicago applied significant pressure against the change. As a result, the state now mandates two levels of service. The transitional bilingual (TBE) program, which requires a bilingual teacher, applies

---

actually spent on those students, as opposed to other students with other special needs.

[15]Reliable data on the actual cost that local districts incur in mounting a supplemental program of instruction for LEP students are limited because of significant variation in the nature of local programs. In a recent study of fifteen school-level programs in California considered to be well-implemented, Chambers and Parrish (1992) found that the marginal cost per pupil ranged from a high of $1,278 in an ESL pull-out program to lows of $235 in a sheltered English class and $241 in a late-exit bilingual program. The other two program models examined, early-exit bilingual and double immersion, had average per-pupil costs of $275 and $956, respectively. However, Chambers and Parrish note that their findings cannot be generalized to other sites or to the state of California as a whole.

Because it uses an excess-cost formula, Illinois has data on the supplemental costs of local programs. In 1990, the average claim for the transitional bilingual program was $1439 per student and for the transitional program of instruction, $814. Included in the excess cost formula are salaries, materials, staff development, and some transportation for pre-K students.

Table 2.1

State Programs for LEP Students
(FY 1990)

	Number of LEP Students	State Funding	Service Requirements
California	849,772 (18.2 percent of all K–12 students)	$100 million Generated by LEP students, but no requirement to spend it on them instead of other disadvantaged students.	There are no specific bilingual requirement after legislative sunset, though original intent is still operative. The intent is to develop English proficiency, and provide access to core curriculum for LEP students.
Florida	83,937 (4.6 percent of all K–12 students)	$132.7 million 0.6 additional ADA	Local districts are required to submit a plan indicating how they will provide intensive English-language and subject-area instruction to LEP students that is understandable to them and comparable in quality to that provided English-proficient students, either in their native language or using ESL techniques. Districts are also required to develop an individual plan for each LEP student.
Illinois	73,000 (4 percent of all K–12 students)	$48.3 million Districts reimbursed 89% of excess cost for salaries, materials, and staff development.	If 20 or more students speak the same language in an *attendance center*, district is required to provide a bilingual teacher (TBE program). If <20, district is required to provide a locally determined transitional program (TPI).

Table 2.1—continued

	Number of LEP Students	State Funding	Service Requirements
New York	122,041 (5 percent of all K–12 students)	$44 million 0.15 additional ADA	If a district wishes to receive state funding, it must provide a bilingual program if 20 or more students speak the same language at a *grade level* in a school building. If <20, only ESL is required.
Texas	308,410 (9 percent of all K–12 students)	$36.5 million 0.1 additional ADA	If 20 or more students speak the same language in a district at the same *grade level*, then district shall offer bilingual/ESL. Bilingual instruction is required in K–6, either bilingual or ESL in 78, ESL in 912. If < 20 students, ESL must be provided.
Virginia	16,277 (2 percent of all K–12 students)	$1.7 million	There are no state regulations or guidelines, but statewide improvement plan for educating LEP and immigrant students are just being implemented. The program focuses on technical assistance and moving towards greater standardization in ESL programs.

to attendance centers with 20 or more students speaking the same language. Where there are fewer than 20 (even if it is only one child), the district must only provide a transitional program of instruction (TPI). This program is locally determined and can use existing staff, peer tutors, or other approaches. However, this program must include native-language instruction to the extent necessary.

The standards now being implemented in Florida take a different approach to district requirements. Rather than specifying the number of students that trigger a particular kind of service, Florida requires that districts submit a plan to the state department of education outlining how they will provide services to LEP students. The parameters within which districts must operate are to provide intensive English-language and subject-matter instruction that is understandable to LEP students and of comparable quality to that provided English speakers. However, districts have some flexibility in the mix between native-language and ESL instruction. Districts are also required to develop an individual plan for each LEP student, outlining the services being provided, and to ensure access to appropriate categorical programs. The agreement also places considerable emphasis on guaranteeing that those teaching LEP students have adequate qualifications. These qualifications include an ESL endorsement (requiring coursework) for teaching basic ESL and in-service requirements for those teaching subject-matter courses through ESL techniques.

Over time, the states have become stricter about the criteria districts must use in admitting students and having them exit from LEP programs. As a result of the *Gomez* decision, Illinois will require a standardized test and is considering using the 50th percentile as the cutoff point. In New York, districts were previously required to serve students scoring below the 23rd percentile. However, as the result of a 1988 change in Board of Regents' policy, the state's bilingual program was expanded. Beginning with the 1990-1991 school year, all students who speak a language other than English at home and score below the 40th percentile on a standardized test of English are to be served. Texas also recently changed its cutoff point for services to language-minority students from the 23rd to the 40th percentile. This change was made because students who had been judged ready to exit local bilingual programs were ending up back in them, as teachers determined that they could not do the work required in mainstream English classes. As a result of the META agreement, Florida now requires that students whose home language is other than English and who score below the 32nd percentile on the reading and writing parts of a norm-referenced test be provided appropriate services.

Prior to the sunset of the bilingual program in California, local districts operated under mandates similar to those in Illinois, New York, and Texas regulating the conditions under which a program had to be offered. Although state requirements have now been loosened, the state monitors local districts under a general framework established by the *Lau* decision and subsequent federal court rulings. The standard used by the state is twofold: Districts have to implement programs to develop English proficiency in LEP students, and LEP students must have access to the core curriculum, even if it means providing instruction in their native language. According to state education department staff, that general intent requires that local districts have programs that are pedagogically effective, taught by qualified personnel, and evaluated on a regular basis. However, the state has had to grant waivers to a number of districts because of the severe shortage of bilingual teachers. While most districts in the state are offering a transitional bilingual program to the extent possible, more and more are having to rely on ESL and sheltered English approaches to instruction.

State governments are in the position of mandating programs that impose considerable service requirements on local districts and providing only modest support for program operations. The states play an even more limited role in building local capacity to accomplish the task of serving language-minority students. The most extensive programs are in Illinois and New York, and even they are nominal. Illinois uses about 5 to 7 percent of the state's bilingual program funding to support the Illinois Resource Center (IRC) whose staff of 15 provides various kinds of technical assistance. Sixty to seventy percent of IRC's work is on-site assistance to local districts that request help in student assessment, teacher training, and curriculum development. IRC has developed strategies for the assessment of language-minority children that rely on multiple instruments, including portfolios. It has also trained about 225 teachers over the past three years to become bilingual and ESL teachers, with a special emphasis on training academic-subject teachers in ESL techniques. The bulk of IRC's services are intended for districts outside Chicago.

In addition to bilingual program funding through the state aid formula, New York also has an $11 million categorical program that is used for teacher training and the enhancement of instructional programs. Part of these funds is used to support 11 Bilingual Technical Assistance Centers around the state, which conduct teacher in-service training and develop curriculum.

The other states, however, are more like California, which has seen its professional staff decrease from 28 (before the legislative sunset) to the current 12. The SDE staff sponsors a statewide conference once a year and has produced a guidebook that focuses on content-based primary-language instruction in each of the state's core curriculum areas. But SDE staff provide almost no on-site technical assistance to districts and have only documented the extent of the severe bilingual teacher shortage, leaving efforts to remedy it entirely to local districts.

Have state mandates worked to ensure that all language-minority children in need of services receive them? That question cannot be answered with any precision, because there are no reliable data on which to base a judgment. However, the continuing success of advocacy groups in pressing lawsuits on behalf of unserved and underserved students attests to the fact that not all language-minority students are being served. The extent of the problem is a matter of dispute in most states, but state department of education staff members readily admit that there are service gaps and that the scope and quality of instruction can vary considerably across districts.

In large measure, that variation is due to differences in local commitment to serving immigrant and other LEP students, a factor that state governments can influence only indirectly through the strength of their mandates, how rigorously they enforce them, and the level of incentives they provide. But variation is also the product of local capacity, a factor over which the states have considerable control if they choose to exercise it. Capacity differences in instruction for language-minority students depend on three factors: funding, qualified personnel, and the process by which students are initially assessed for program eligibility and their subsequent progress is monitored. States vary considerably in the extent to which they have decided to assist districts in bearing the additional costs associated with educating LEP students. For example, Illinois pays the bulk of these costs (about 75 percent in 1991), while in California, local districts must bear the overwhelming majority of costs from their general fund budgets.[16] States have documented the lack of qualified personnel, and some have begun to provide training resources, largely to equip practicing teachers with the skills to use ESL and sheltered-English instructional strategies. But, on the whole, the burden of recruiting and training qualified personnel falls on local districts. Variation in the manner and frequency with which local districts assess language-minority students remains a problem, and efforts to encourage the standardization of procedures are currently under way by the Council of Chief State School Officers (Cheung and Solomon, 1991). That Florida, New York, and Texas decided to use relatively high cut-off points on a norm-referenced test of English reflects the movement to standardize and to be more inclusive of students needing assistance. However, lack of standardization and the ensuing differences across localities in access to LEP programs remains a problem. For example, in their study of 15 exemplary sites in California, Berman and his colleagues (1992) found that only two schools tested LEP students on a regular basis; several schools used a different test for exit than for entrance into the program; and some even used different procedures for exit than for entry (e.g., teacher judgment as opposed to a standardized achievement test).

In sum, while the data are not precise, there is considerable evidence that state mandates have not ensured that all language-minority children in need of services are receiving them. Some of the service gaps can be remedied by more precise and uniformly enforced mandates with regard to student assessment and monitoring. But most will require a higher level of resources and greater state effort (e.g., in working with teacher-training institutions and in sponsoring aggres-

---

[16]Although the nature of the sample does not allow generalization to all districts across the state, Chambers and Parrish (1992) found in their study of 15 local sites that, on average, 87.9 percent of the funds for designated LEP classrooms come from local general funds, with state supplemental monies covering about 5 percent of the costs, and the remainder coming from federal sources.

sive recruiting of bilingual teachers) than most state governments are able or willing to expend at this time. Nevertheless, the variation in program frameworks across states attests to their importance in creating necessary, though not sufficient, conditions for local instructional programs. LEP students in Illinois are more likely to be able to take college-preparatory courses in their native language than counterparts in Virginia, not just because of the greater availability of bilingual teachers in one place than another. The fact that Illinois requires that classes for language-minority students be taught by bilingual teachers and Virginia does not sets a standard to which local districts must strive and against which they can be monitored.

CHAPTER CONCLUSIONS

The federal role in immigrant education is programmatically limited. Expenditures specifically targeted for immigrant students are minuscule, and the more substantial investment from Title VII programs serves only a fraction of recent immigrants. Yet the legal framework established as a result of the *Lau* decision has been influential in shaping the kind of language instruction that immigrant students receive. That framework has been the major basis on which groups representing language-minority students have pressured state governments into providing additional services for those students. It has also meant that the problems of immigrant students are rarely considered independent of their need to learn English, and to the extent that immigrant education is a visible policy issue, it bears all the emotional baggage of the highly controversial politics of bilingual education.

From the federal perspective, then, the dilemma of immigrant education is defined by two factors. The localized impact of immigration means that the federal government has little incentive to address the unique needs of newcomers. On the other hand, the aspect of those students' schooling requirements most likely to gain widespread attention—their need to learn English—is so intertwined with fundamental cultural and political beliefs that it is rarely addressed as solely an educational issue.

By default, our discussion of state policy has also focused on that level of government's role in educating language-minority students. Independent of their need to learn English and to escape the consequences of poverty, immigrant students are not viewed by state poli-cymakers as a distinct group requiring unique policy remedies. Even in California, where immigrants have profoundly changed the state's schools over the past decade, policymakers see immigrant students as children who need to learn English, to be provided the medical and social services in short supply for all poor children, and to be given the academic and social resources to stay in school. That im-migrants may have different needs from those of native-born stu-dents is neither widely recognized nor accepted.

Politically, the invisibility of immigrant education may be a mixed blessing. On the one hand, state policymakers' perceptions of immi-grant youth as students living in poverty who need to learn English mean that they are the beneficiaries of well-established programs for LEP students and programs for poor students, such as free lunches. Immigrant students are also part of the group to which recently pro-posed reforms, such as the coordinated delivery of social services at the school site, are directed. On the other hand, immigrant students' low visibility has meant that they are at the mercy of whatever the current politics of bilingual education are and, perhaps more impor-tantly, receive no special state funding for services specific to their status as newcomers (e.g., psychological counseling to help in over-coming the stresses of adjusting to a new culture).

The alternative to immigrant education's current status on state policy agendas would be to single out and recognize immigrant stu-dents as a group with needs not completely met by current categori-cal programs. The advantage of this alternative is that any policies enacted on their behalf would more likely be appropriate to immi-grant needs. However, there is a distinct political risk involved in making the unique needs of immigrant students visible at the state level. That risk can be described in one simple word: backlash. The current political debate about whether immigrants are net producers or net consumers of public services is one that may become more strident, particularly if the American economy remains weak.

The potential payoff from policies that would provide immigrant students with more appropriate services versus the risk of creating a widespread backlash is the dilemma that advocates for immigrant children face in planning future strategies. For the present, however, the federal and state roles in immigrant education remain limited, with the responsibility for serving these students falling largely on local districts and schools.

In the next chapter, we examine how eight districts with large numbers of immigrant students are responding to their needs.

Chapter Three

SCHOOL DISTRICTS RESPOND TO IMMIGRATION

In this chapter, we examine the problems faced by the eight districts in our study sample as they have attempted to meet the schooling needs of immigrant students. We found that most teachers and administrators who work with immigrants view them positively and are making a valiant effort to educate them in a caring manner. Yet their good intentions do not always translate into effective services for immigrant students, largely because most of these districts lack the human and fiscal resources to educate students well, whether they are immigrant or native born.

The chapter has four sections. We first review the challenges facing school systems that educate large numbers of immigrant students and, second, describe the services provided immigrant students in our sample districts. A third section discusses the unmet educational and social needs of immigrant children, and the concluding section outlines the main themes that emerge from our analysis.

CHALLENGES

Student Characteristics

As the discussion in Chapter One indicated, immigrant students are a diverse group. In the largest cities, they represent as many as 100 different countries; even though the majority speak Spanish, they hail from a variety of different cultures.

The one common characteristic of most immigrant children is poverty. Although some middle-class immigrant families have fled political unrest (particularly Cubans and Haitians to Miami and

Eastern Europeans and Central Asians to New York and Chicago), most recent immigrants have come seeking better economic opportunities. The vast majority are from very poor countries and are themselves from the poorest segments of those societies. Like the Europeans who came to America in the late 19th and early 20th centuries, the majority of immigrant families sending children to public schools are destitute; the only capital they bring is their courage and willingness to work. Among the districts we studied, the only outlier in this respect is Fairfax, in which a sizable minority of immigrants are from middle class, diplomatic, or professional families.

Other demographic characteristics of immigrants are also important in defining the problems that school systems must solve. One is concentration: Foreign-born students constitute about one-fifth of the school populations in Los Angeles, Miami, and San Francisco. New York City would fit the same category if Puerto Ricans, who are American citizens but Spanish speakers, were counted as immigrants. In contrast, Chicago, Houston, and Fairfax are all districts in which the overwhelming majority of students are native born and English speaking. In all the districts but Fairfax and Visalia, the majority of native-born students are low and middle income African Americans.

A related demographic characteristic of immigrants is location. Immigrant groups in some cities live in well-established barrios or other ethnic neighborhoods that offer low-cost housing and social support. But the size and diversity of the immigrant population have created new housing patterns. In Los Angeles, Fairfax, and Miami, Hispanic immigrants are so numerous that they now settle outside of traditional barrios, in older neighborhoods that were until recently exclusively Anglo. In New York, Chicago, and Miami, immigrant groups from new source countries are establishing their own settlement neighborhoods. The Sweetwater area of Miami, once all white Anglo, is now predominantly Nicaraguan, and the Eastern part of Hialeah is newly a Haitian neighborhood. In New York, parts of Brooklyn and Queens have become home to Russian, Afghan, and Kurdish groups whose numbers have grown dramatically in recent years.

As subsequent sections of this chapter will show, these demographic characteristics are a key factor in shaping how school systems have tried to change their staffing and course offerings to serve immigrant students.

District Resources

Funding. As this is written, all of the districts, including relatively affluent Fairfax, are suffering major cutbacks in funding. Los Angeles' total funding fell nearly 20 percent between September 1990 and January 1992. Chicago faced a $220 million deficit in 1991–1992, on a $2.4 billion budget. Chicago's annual deficit is expected to exceed $500 million within 5 years. New York City and Dade County face years of deficits approaching 10 percent of their projected budgets.

All the districts are suspending or abandoning activities that their boards had considered essential elements of program quality. The cuts have immediate effects on student services. Los Angeles, Houston, and New York have increased pupil-teacher ratios, and New York has cut costs by furloughing teachers and students for periods during the school year. Miami has slowed the construction of schools in overflow areas. All districts have cut back on maintenance and repairs. Chicago's central office, already cut by a school-centered reform movement, will face even deeper reductions due to the budget deficit. Chicago will also further defer an estimated $1 billion in critically needed maintenance and repairs, continue a freeze on teacher hiring, and increase class size in all schools. All districts report overcrowding of schools, especially in immigrant neighborhoods. All the districts have reduced extracurricular activities and supportive after-school services. Most Los Angeles schools have gone to year-round schedules. New York has suspended special training programs designed to help immigrant professionals become bilingual and ESL teachers, and all districts have curtailed the hiring of replacement teachers. Fairfax has eliminated the merit-pay plan for high-performing teachers that was the centerpiece of the superintendent's educational reform strategy.

Although the fiscal crisis is universal, its consequences are different in Fairfax and Visalia than in the big cities. In Fairfax, many programs have been cut, but the district remains one of the country's best-staffed and most-respected school systems. Visalia also has problems, but it is able to take new initiatives and to continue improving its schools. In these districts, unlike Los Angeles, Chicago, and New York, the quality of schooling for native-born students is good, if not ideal.

As Chapter Two details, all the districts we studied have some special resources to help schools cope with the added expense and complexity of education for non–English-speaking students. These resources are of three kinds: general revenue assistance from the state or federal governments, based on formulas taking account of the excess costs of educating an LEP student; local state and federal categorical programs that subsidize specific services for eligible LEP students; and state and federal grants for supplementary services to disadvantaged students, which can be used to strengthen programs in schools with large numbers of immigrants. However, in most cases, these special programs pay less than half of the excess cost of educating language-minority students.

Teachers. Respondents in every district said that they were unable to place all immigrant students in classrooms with teachers who spoke their native language. In some districts, this problem affects relatively few students, e.g., Haitians and Southern Europeans in Miami and Russians in Chicago. But most districts reported having trouble finding teachers even for the Hispanic students, who are most prevalent everywhere. Only Miami, with a very large supply of middle-class Cuban-American teachers, has no real shortage of Spanish-speaking teachers. Even Los Angeles, which offers a $5,000 annual salary incentive for bilingual teachers, is frequently unable to match Spanish-speaking immigrants with Spanish-speaking teachers. With few exceptions, districts are unable to provide teachers who speak Creole French, Arabic languages, central Asian languages, Russian, or Asian languages other than Japanese or Chinese.

Most of the districts are able to hire some bilingual aides—immigrants or U.S.-born adults who speak the children's home languages but who do not have teaching credentials. Some of these aides are well educated and can substitute effectively for teachers, while others have little education and can provide only custodial care and rough translation. Because these aides are paid much less than teachers and frequently do not get full employee benefits, school systems find it easy to employ them. Some immigrant groups, fearing that use of aides instead of teachers will become permanent, have threatened to sue over inequities in the quality of teachers provided immigrant and native-born children.

Though teachers who can speak immigrant students' native languages are in short supply, many districts are unable to hire new ones even when they become available. The general hiring freezes caused by budget deficits apply equally to bilingual and monolingual teachers. In cities with hiring freezes (e.g., in New York and Chicago), incumbent teachers' seniority rights also make it difficult to change the staffing of schools when neighborhoods become immigrant settlement areas.

Books and Curricula. The second shortage particular to immigrant education is instructional materials—textbooks, stories and novels, histories and biographies, curriculum guides, filmstrips, and tests. Although such materials are in good supply for Spanish-speaking students, they are seldom available for other language groups. American publishers have not found a large enough market to justify developing materials in many languages, and no public agency at the local, state, or federal level has invested in the necessary research and development. This shortage affects student assessment and placement, as well as classroom teaching. Educators at all levels, from central office administrators to classroom teachers, said that there are few good instruments for assessing an LEP student's general academic development or mastery of English.

As some local respondents told us, materials from students' native countries are often of little use because they presume a mastery of the native language that few U.S. teachers have. Many educators have, however, expressed a desire for analyses of the curricula and instructional materials used in source countries to help teachers tailor their instruction to match their students' preparation. Few such analyses are available. U.S. teachers of non–Spanish-speaking immigrant children are forced to use standard English-language texts and materials, whatever their students' language backgrounds and academic preparation.

Competing Demands

The dramatic growth in immigration in the 1980s has greatly increased the number and proportion of immigrant students in the schools. Many of the large urban districts we studied bucked a national trend of declining enrollments, entirely because of immigration. Even in Los Angeles and Dade County, where foreign-born students had been present in large numbers for decades, the recent waves of immigration have made enormous changes. Despite these changes, however, immigrants are not the only disadvantaged group demanding the districts' attention. With the exceptions of Fairfax and Visalia, all the districts we studied are "majority minority." African Americans constitute the majority of all students in Chicago and are strongly represented in all the other cities. Latinos represent over half the student population in Los Angeles and close to half in Houston; Puerto Ricans make up nearly 40 percent of the New York population; and Asian-Americans of various nationalities are nearly half of all the students in San Francisco.

With the exception of the San Francisco Asians, all the nonimmigrant minority groups served by the city school systems we visited are experiencing major educational difficulties. Even in our smaller districts, Fairfax and Visalia, native-born minority students fare much worse than their Anglo classmates. In the big-city systems, the problem is much more severe. They have plainly failed to attract, motivate, and hold the Puerto Rican, African American, and Mexican American students who are their primary clientele.

Coupled with the financial problems discussed above, this phenomenon of general educational failure in the big cities means that the school systems are not able to concentrate enormous human or financial resources on immigrants alone. Board members and administrators must either split their attention in many directions or develop strategies that improve the schools' general capacity to educate.

Table 3.1 summarizes board members' and superintendents' responses to questions about the gravest problems facing their districts. Even though all respondents thought immigration posed major challenges (and knew that this study was particularly focused on the problem of immigrant education), they identified problems in broad terms: The districts are profoundly troubled and are finding it difficult to provide sound educational experiences to any of their students.

Table 3.1

Top Three Constraints on Services to Immigrants by District, in Order of Priority

	LA	SF	V	H	D	NY	C	F
Budget crisis	1	1	1	1	1	1	1	1
Space, crowding	2		2		2		2	
Shortage of staff (bilingual or ESL)	3	2	3	2		2		2
Instructional materials		3				3		
Social & health services				3	3		3	3

Top officials in most districts named systemic problems, budget and space, as the primary constraints on good education for immigrant children. They attached great importance to needs specific to immigrant education, particularly teachers and health services. But the systemic problems, which now hamper the education of all students in the big cities, are more fundamental. Solving them does not guarantee good education for immigrant children, but fiscal health and classroom space are clearly preconditions.

These problems are especially severe for the large urban districts. Though the smaller suburban and rural districts face competing demands and painful trade-offs, the big-city districts are vastly more complex, in administrative structures, constituency politics, labor management relations, and financing. Taken together, these problems set the big-city districts apart, as facing problems far greater than their capacities to cope.

The rural and suburban districts, in contrast, are being forced to make difficult changes and adjustments, but they still have the capacity to cope and adapt to the challenges posed by immigration.

SERVICES TO IMMIGRANT CHILDREN

Attitudes and Intentions

The discussion that follows in the remainder of the chapter obscures a central fact about most schools' services to immigrant children.

The vast majority of immigrant schools are happy bustling places, filled with eager children and adults who take great pleasure in working with them. The xenophobia that characterizes much public discussion about preservation of the English language and protection of American workers' jobs does not pervade these schools.

Immigrant students are treated as children—highly sympathetic children who need help but are also open, willing to work, and rewarding to those who teach them. Immigrant education is flexible and fast moving. New children enter school every day, and different children progress at strikingly different rates. School principals and teachers who love routine cannot last in immigrant schools. The students' needs and their eagerness either break through a reluctant teacher's reserve or deplete his energies.

Teachers speak vividly of their work with immigrant students. The researchers who visited schools for this project can easily see why. The experiences of watching 16-year-old Asian boys learn the names for pencil and paper in the New York newcomer school and of trying to walk down a Dade County primary school hallway when 1,200 knee-high children were moving toward their classrooms were unforgettable. So was the experience of one research team member who was smothered with kisses from tiny 6-year old African American, Cuban, Nicaraguan, Haitian, and Salvadoran first graders in a Liberty City, Miami, classroom. The principals and teachers who learn the names of every child in their class in two days are doing real work, but the rewards are great. As one Los Angeles principal said, "Our teachers never leave. Once they start teaching immigrants they don't want to stop. They enjoy being valued. Immigrants respect teachers and education."

Immigrant children are, in fact, uncommonly rewarding. Teacher comments from a sample of Los Angeles students' cumulative records confirm the interview responses we obtained elsewhere. As Table 3.2 shows, a significantly greater proportion of new immigrant students (those in the United States for less than three years) are considered well motivated and "bright" than are native-born students or more established immigrants. Los Angeles transcript data also show that immigrant elementary school students have better attendance records than their American-born or more established

Table 3.2

**Los Angeles Elementary School Teachers' Assessment of Student Attitudes
(Coded from teacher comments on students' cumulative files)**

| | | Type of Student | | |
Students Considered:	Native-Born	Established Immigrant	New Immigrant	Significance
Well-motivated	25%	35%	61%	a
Bright, fast learner	13%	16%	29%	b
Good social behavior	20%	11%	24%	ns
Good classroom behavior	7%	8%	12%	ns
Number of student files	153	80	49	

[a]Differences significant at 0.01 level.
[b]Significant at 0.05 level.
ns—not statistically significant.

immigrant classmates. These patterns do not, however, persist long after immigration. As some teachers told us ruefully, immigrant students Americanize all too soon. But in the first few years they are especially rewarding pupils.

The following catalogue of problems and trials can be truly understood only in light of these facts about the joy and optimism that immigrant students and their teachers share.

District Organization

Do school districts recognize immigrant students as a distinctive clientele that needs special attention? Is anybody specifically assigned to ensure that immigrant students get what they need? Are the staff members responsible for immigrant education highly enough placed to ensure that students' needs are seriously considered in the allocation of district resources? We attempted to answer these questions in the sample districts.

All of the districts in the study organized their services to immigrants under the general heading of bilingual-LEP education. All the districts have coordinators of bilingual education, who historically administered federal and state grants for LEP students and acted as local compliance officers in relations with the state department of education, the federal Office for Civil Rights, and the courts. Coordinators of bilingual education also typically hire and train teachers and aides who specialize in bilingual education and English as a Second Language (ESL), administer local procedures for allocating those teachers among schools, and provide assistance to principals and regular classroom teachers in schools with LEP students.

In some of our districts, immigrant education is treated simply as language education, and no clear distinctions are drawn between programs for native-born LEP students and for immigrants. Five of our districts, however, make careful distinctions between native-born and immigrant students and are organized accordingly.

The one organizational characteristic that distinguishes the two types of district is the existence of an immigrant student intake center. The three California districts, Dade, and Fairfax, have built organizations specifically dedicated to proper placement of new immigrant students. These organizations test every incoming foreign born student on English-language proficiency and general educational development. Multilingual placement specialists allocate immigrant students to schools, ensuring that as many as possible will have access to teachers who speak their native languages. The centers also hire and assign circuit-riding consultants, who can keep track of students who speak low-incidence languages. These consultants review students' educational progress and can recommend supplementary programs or changes in school placement.

The other districts in our sample have no such placement or consulting organizations. An immigrant student appears in the neighborhood school and receives whatever service the school can offer. The immigrant student intake centers are far from perfect; teachers in every district complained that their assessments of students' language and skills development were often flawed. Centers dealing with multiple language groups were particularly prone to errors. But the alternative, informal assessments done by overworked teachers at the school site, are apparently much worse. Such centers are essential if a district intends to assign immigrant students individually to the schools best equipped to meet their needs.

The districts without immigrant student-placement centers make few distinctions between native-born LEP students, such as Puerto Ricans and second-generation Mexican-Americans, and children who are themselves immigrants. In New York City, for example, the structure and content of bilingual-LEP services were designed for Puerto Ricans, who once were the overwhelming majority of non–English-speaking students. Today's immigrant students are, however, unlike Puerto Ricans in important ways: They are not American citizens and are seldom connected with well-assimilated, economically established, and politically organized groups of earlier immigrants.

There are two important organizational differences between districts whose LEP students are mostly immigrants and those whose LEP students are mostly native born. First, immigrant-oriented districts are more likely to be concerned about issues of acculturation, social-welfare services, and adult education. Immigrant-oriented school systems, as in the case of Miami, are often staffed by people who were immigrants themselves and are therefore keenly aware of the social and emotional adjustments that must be made as students enter American schools. Dade County Superintendent Octavio Visiedo, for example, was himself an immigrant, a member of the Peter Pan Brigade, a group of children who preceded their families to Miami shortly after Castro took power in Cuba in 1959. Many other members of the Dade County central office staff, and thousands of teachers and principals, were also born in Cuba.

School system central offices that are specifically oriented toward immigrants are likely to take an assimilationist approach to education, orienting school services toward understanding of local community institutions and labor markets and helping students make the quickest possible transition to the use of English.

Other school system offices, particularly in New York, Chicago, and Houston, are more likely to define their services purely in terms of language. In these places, tensions between immigrant and native LEP perspectives are apparent. Efforts to expand social services, provide extensive classwork on local history and institutions, and expand education for immigrant parents compete for resources with efforts to enhance bilingual education and support students' continued use of their native languages.

The tensions are most apparent in New York City, where services to LEP students are governed by the ASPIRA consent decree.[1] In that decree, the public school system promises to provide bilingual education indefinitely to any LEP student who cannot score above a set level on an English-language test of academic skills.

Yet in New York, as in most other school systems with large numbers of immigrants, teachers who speak any foreign language other than Spanish are in short supply. The consent decree is, therefore, virtually a dead issue for students from Africa, Asia, central and southern Europe, and the Middle East. The city's bilingual education office concentrates on abiding by the consent decree whenever it can. Consequently, Spanish-speaking students, whether immigrant or native born, are assured of substantial bilingual education, while students from other language groups get neither bilingual education nor significant help with acculturation.

In Dade County, the discrepancies between services for Spanish-speaking and other LEP students are also considerable. As in New York, there are few teachers who speak other languages. However, because the Dade County central office is specifically oriented toward immigrant education, supplementary acculturation coursework, social services, and adult outreach education are more accessible to all language groups.

Throughout the country, state and local education agencies are reluctant to create organizations specifically dedicated to immigrant education. Funds are too short to support a major new organizational focus. But funding is not the only issue. Even in Fairfax, by far the best funded of our school systems, no organization is specifically

---

[1]The ASPIRA consent decree, and other legal settlements affecting services to LEP students in the districts we studied (e.g., the META decree in Florida, discussed below), are all roughly based on the *Lau* principles advocated by the U.S. Office for Civil Rights. The *Lau* principles hold that a foreign-born or native LEP student should be instructed in her native language until two conditions are met: First, the student demonstrates no significant impairment in reading, writing, and speaking English, and second, that the student's achievement in English-language tests of academic skills be at or near the average for students of her age. Unlike many local school-district policies, *Lau* does not establish a minimum or a maximum number of years that students should receive bilingual education. It relies instead on student performance criteria and imposes an open-ended obligation on districts to provide bilingual education until those criteria are met.

dedicated to immigrants. Many political leaders resist making a structural change in response to what might be a transitory phenomenon.

Instruction

Immigrant students pose a number of issues, some obvious and others less apparent, to the schools that serve them. The first and most obvious is language. The vast majority do not speak English, and although the majority of all immigrants speak Spanish, some school systems serve immigrants who speak many different languages. New York, Chicago, Los Angeles, and Fairfax all have at least 20 students from each of more than 100 language groups.

The second issue is academic preparation. Some children appear at school unprepared for the subjects usually taught to students of their age. Students of all ages and from all language groups can suffer from this problem. It is, however, most pronounced among older children, especially those of junior high and high school age, from war-torn areas and economically underdeveloped regions. Because a great deal of immigration has been caused by economic desperation (particularly in Mexico) and by war or revolution (e.g., in Haiti, Central America, Southeast Asia, the Middle East, and Africa), a high proportion of all immigrant students arrive in the United States with serious educational deficiencies. Although such distress has always been common among immigrants, officials in all districts report that more students are educationally unprepared, and their educational deficits are more severe, than ever before. As a Los Angeles principal said:

> A third of the Hispanic students have never been to school before they arrive here; about 80 percent of the Hispanic students have been separated from their parents for about five to eight years (the children are either sent here to live with relatives or they are left behind in their native country for some years while their parents come to the U.S. to look for work). The other students come to LA with their families and most of them have had some prior schooling. The Filipino students usually have more English skills than the other students.

The third issue is mobility. Immigration does not respect the school calendar. Students arrive in schools at all times of year. Because immigrant families typically change places of residence frequently— doubling or tripling up with other families until the adults get regular jobs and then moving to less-crowded accommodations each time the family income increases—schools serving immigrant students must cope with very high rates of turnover. A San Francisco principal said:

> Every year there are changes in the student population, either the languages spoken or level of academic preparation. Staff make plans at the end of each year for curriculum modifications and improvement for the next year, but when fall arrives, the needs of the students who actually enroll may necessitate different instructional strategies and materials.

A Miami principal commented:

> The influx of students at many different times makes it difficult for us to plan our lessons successfully. Bilingual curriculum content classes are now overloaded even though they were relatively empty at the beginning of the school year.

Some of the schools we studied had turnover rates near 100 percent, that is, twice as many students were enrolled in the school at some time during the school year than were enrolled on any given day. The majority of schools in our surveys had turnover rates over 50 percent.

Some immigrant students who do not move from one school to another nonetheless disappear for long periods in the academic year. Principals and teachers in Los Angeles, Houston, Miami, and New York City reported that many immigrant families from western-hemisphere countries take children out of school for weeks and months at a time for visits home. One Los Angeles principal noted, "Around December parents go off for the holidays and take their kids. There is a big exodus then. . . . In the past two weeks, 30 students have come back and 10 have left."

Most such absences begin during the Christmas holidays, and may often extend into March or even April. Families who can return home over land are particularly likely to take children out of schools in Los Angeles and Houston. As educators in New York and Miami reported, wholesale student absences begin as soon as airlines announce their winter discount fares.

Many immigrant families apparently do not share or understand U.S. expectations about uninterrupted school attendance. Despite their obvious desire to live in the United States, they retain expectations for educational work and attainment derived from their home cultures.

This leads to the fourth issue, which is the general difficulty of adjustment to the United States. The rigors of immigration, especially over land from Mexico and central America, by sea from Haiti, or through refugee camps in Kurdestan and Southeast Asia, leave many children exhausted and ill. Many immigrant students also suffer from severe emotional stress. One principal told of several extreme cases:

> When we see children who are suicidal or suffering from insomnia, there's always a reason. For example, one child saw his father killed. One girl couldn't stop shivering because she witnessed her uncle mutilated and killed. Her aunt then remarried and her second husband killed her—the violence continues. We had a boy here who was being carried by his grandmother when she was shot; there was blood all over him.

Most of the children who enter the United States from Mexico, Central America, and Asia endure family separations in the course of immigration. In many cases, children immigrate only after one or both parents have spent time in the United States finding work and living quarters. In one California school we visited, a ten-year-old girl had just been reunited with her mother after an eight-year separation. Children frequently immigrate only to join families that have been permanently split by divorce or the decision of one parent to return to the home country. Even intact families are frequently disrupted by parents' emotional distress and their need to work multiple jobs. Again, although schools resist becoming social-service agencies and dispensers of family therapy, they must often reach out to families to ensure that children come to school rested and calm enough to learn.

The remainder of this section explores how schools try to resolve four issues: language-appropriate instruction, poor academic preparation, mobility, and social adjustment. It identifies general patterns of service and calls attention to especially significant differences among the districts studied.

Language and Instruction. Throughout the 1970s and 1980s, a debate raged over the relative merits of bilingual education, i.e., teaching in the native language until the student had become completely fluent in English, and of English as a Second Language (ESL), teaching that relies almost entirely on English to convey academic materials and to promote language acquisition. At the core of the debate was a difference of opinion (fueled by competing research findings) about what method led students to learn the most in the long run. But the contending sides also differed on the desirability of supporting students' continued use and mastery of their native languages (e.g., see Crawford, 1991; Hakuta, 1986; Willig, 1985).

Remnants of the debate are still evident in school systems' services to language-minority students. But the logic of necessity is overwhelming in most cases. In general, school systems offer at least some bilingual education to new immigrant students whenever possible. But the needs of students who speak no English are so great that few school systems are able to offer any native-language instruction to students who are even moderately competent in English. There are, furthermore, many language groups for whom the school systems are able to hire very few teachers. Students who speak these languages are often taught exclusively by monolingual English-speaking teachers. Children who speak low-incidence languages often attend schools where an ESL class can contain students from as many as ten different language groups.

Table 3.3 summarizes the relative emphasis on bilingual and ESL instruction in the school systems. It reflects the fact that most systems offer bilingual instruction only to the largest language groups and emphasize ESL for smaller groups and later arrivals. Most districts, furthermore, minimize the use of bilingual education in high schools, trying to ensure that students obtain access to substantive courses that are only taught in English. Only Fairfax county relies exclusively on ESL.

Table 3.3

Principal Approach to Language Instruction for Non-English Speakers, by Native Language

Language Group	Bilingual[a]	ESL
Spanish	D, LA, SF, V, H, C, NY	F
Asian	SF, NY, LA, C	D, C, H, F, V
East European	NY, C	C, D, F, LA
Middle Eastern		D, NY, F, C, LA
African		NY, F, D
French	NY	F, D
Other European	NY, D, LA, C	F, H, SF

[a]Some districts offer limited bilingual or immersion programs in lower-incidence languages. Chicago, for example, offers limited numbers of bilingual programs in Cantonese, Vietnamese, Korean, Russian, Indo-Pakistani, and Polish. New York offers Russian, Polish, Cantonese, and Korean in some schools. Fairfax offers Japanese, Spanish, and French immersion programs, and Miami offers one sequence of classes in Italian. Most immigrants speaking the languages listed above, however, receive only ESL instruction.

Fairfax does provide limited numbers of immersion programs in Spanish, French, and Japanese. But these programs are meant to attract middle-class English speakers and English-speaking foreign-born students, not to serve as an instructional model for the large numbers of non–English-speaking immigrant students. Fairfax allocates extra teaching slots to immigrant schools, and the schools can decide when to hire bilingual teachers or simply to reduce class size for all students. Whenever possible, students from low-incidence language groups are assigned to schools that have at least some staff members that speak their language. But most such students are in schools that have only monolingual-English or English and Spanish-speaking teachers.

None of the districts that provide bilingual education pursue a consistent language-maintenance approach for immigrant students. Some, particularly San Francisco, Miami, and New York, try to make home-language instruction available as long as possible. The Miami school board also favors teaching and maintaining second languages for all students, including native English speakers. But all districts have been forced to put scarce bilingual manpower where it is most desperately needed, with new immigrants who speak little or no English.

Respondents in all the districts explained that their choices between bilingual and ESL modes of instruction are dictated by teacher supply. With the exception of Hispanics, Chinese, Poles, and Russians, most recent immigrant groups do not bring qualified teachers with them. Nor do such groups as the Hmong, Afghans, Kurds, and Haitians have large numbers of U.S.–resident teachers who can speak their languages. Although several of the urban systems have hired aides who speak immigrant students' languages, school systems serving students from such groups have no choice but to offer them ESL instruction.

All districts have developed techniques for stretching the supply of bilingual teachers as far as it can go. Fairfax and Miami employ bilingual consultants who work as circuit riders, visiting the schools where immigrant students are being taught by ESL teachers who do not speak their languages. These consulting teachers work as casework advocates for individual students, and also advise regular classroom teachers on methods of helping immigrant students. Miami also provides a special category of courses called *bilingual curriculum content* (BCC). These courses are team-taught by an English-speaking subject-matter specialist (e.g., in mathematics or science) and a bilingual teacher who is not a subject-matter specialist. The bilingual teacher explains key concepts in the students' native language and alerts the content teacher when immigrant students' interest or comprehension is falling off. BCC classes were evident in every Miami school we visited, at all levels from early elementary grades through high school. Even schools with large numbers of bilingual teachers had some BCC classes.

Districts that have significant numbers of bilingual teachers but cannot keep up with the continual growth of the immigrant population, such as Houston, are often unable to provide extensive bilingual instruction. But they do try to give each immigrant student a "home base" in the school, with at least one teacher who speaks the native language. This is most often accomplished by assigning students to a Spanish-speaking homeroom. Though some critics have condemned the resulting isolation of immigrant students, the teachers and principals we interviewed claimed that such students feel more secure in the school and adapt more quickly to ESL and pure English-language instruction.

Other districts with a smaller supply of bilingual teachers than Miami's often provide ESL specialists to teach mathematics, science, and social studies. As a Houston principal said:

> Five years ago we [started trying] to set aside a class other than English that could be taught using the ESL methodology. We started with science, then added history, and math was last.

Teachers in such classes may not speak the immigrant students' home languages, but they understand how students acquire new languages and teach in ways that both convey course content and increase English proficiency. This means that they provide concrete examples and definitions to help students learn the English names for important objects and ideas, and they use demonstrations to define verbs. Some also learn key verbs in the students' home languages so they can show how concepts that the students already understand can be translated into English. This description generally fits classes that Los Angeles calls *sheltered English*.[2]

ESL is an elastic term, and it sometimes simply means instruction provided by an English-speaking teacher. But most ESL teachers use techniques of demonstration and definition to convey the meaning of English instruction to non–English-speaking students. Teachers formally trained in ESL have a repertoire of techniques for instructing non–English-speaking students, and even those who have learned ESL on the job tend to have definite approaches to conveying content in English.

Though many of the schools we studied serve immigrant students from only one language group, some have students speaking as many as ten languages. In Fairfax, New York, and San Francisco, schools with five to seven language groups are common. Many of the

---

[2]The state of California now issues certification for teachers teaching sheltered English classes. It is called a Language Development Certificate (LDC) and is less demanding in its requirements than a bilingual credential. The LDC does not require bilingualism and emphasizes language-development skills. It is designed, in the face of bilingual-teacher shortages and the growing number of LEP students, to ensure that monolingual, English-speaking teachers can more effectively teach LEP students.

groups are small, so that none have as many as 20 members per grade. In such cases it is usually impossible for the school to provide any same-language teachers for some students. One Fairfax elementary school we visited contains ten language groups. It provided half-day bilingual instruction for Hispanic and Korean students, but it had no staff members who could speak Kurdish, Arabic, Hmong, or any of the five other languages that students spoke at home. The principal reported an incident in which she was able to resolve a fight between two boys only after bringing five other children to her office to translate among the combatants and herself.

When we asked teachers and principals how they would help immigrant students succeed in U.S. schools, virtually all said that they need greater exposure to instruction in their native languages. Although few argued that schools are responsible for helping students maintain a lifelong competence in their native languages, most asserted that basic-skills learning occurs faster if students are taught bilingually.

Still, many teachers and principals argued that current methods can be effective in teaching students English and increasing academic content knowledge. Most thought that immigrant students who entered American schools at or near grade level could catch up, in terms of basic substantive understanding, within two or three years. Some noted, however, that written expression is very slow to develop. Whether an immigrant student is taught bilingually or via ESL, his or her capacity to write sharply and convey complex ideas clearly in English lags many years behind the rest of her development. As one Dade County middle school teacher said,

> You can be taken in by how bright and responsive the kids are, and they can do pretty well on multiple-choice tests and homework. But anything that requires writing or public speaking throws them. It is like they go back several years.

Teachers repeatedly complained that district-level testing was inaccurate, and that students who were placed at one level often could not perform at that level and had to be reassigned by the school. Although many districts have formal testing programs to assess students' English-language skills (e.g., New York's Language Assessment Battery), many teachers apparently preferred constructing their own.

In Fairfax County, the practice of informal testing is well established: The local student intake center uses locally made tests, and students' placements depend heavily on the tester's judgment. Students' movements from one level of ESL instruction to another, or from ESL to mainstream English-language instruction, also depend primarily on teacher judgment.

Our Los Angeles student transcript data confirm that formal testing of immigrant students' English-language skills is not performed systematically. An analysis of transcripts from one school in that study indicated that 70 percent of its tenth grade ESL students had taken at least two language tests in the course of their two years at the school. In an otherwise similar Los Angeles high school, only 25 percent of the ESL students had been tested more than once.

Deficient Academic Preparation. The instruction provided in standard content areas—reading, spelling, grammar, literature, mathematics, science, social studies, and art—differs depending on the students' age and prior academic attainment. In elementary schools, the majority of immigrant students take standard English-language courses in core subjects within two years of entering the United States. Students who enter in kindergarten, first, or second grades normally gain access to regular instruction well before they leave elementary school, whatever their level of prior academic experience.

Most school systems expect teachers to adjust their instructional methods and content to the needs of first-year immigrant students. After the first year, however, students are introduced to more and more regular classes. Even those new immigrants who receive special bilingual or ESL instruction spend more than half their school day in the same classes as their native-born peers. Elementary-level students who have mastered some English typically take science, social studies, and physical education in regular classes. In Fairfax County, where the school system does not provide bilingual education as a matter of policy, second-year immigrant students are usually placed into regular mathematics and language arts classes as well.

The instruction given older immigrant students depends profoundly on their academic preparation. Immigrants who enter elementary school at grade three or above can have serious problems catching up with regular instruction. Whether this happens in a particular case depends primarily on the student's social class and country of origin. Students who have attended school full time in their native countries are often ahead of American students, especially in mathematics and science. However, students whose schooling was delayed or disrupted due to poverty and war are often far behind. As we saw in many junior high and high schools, some students from rural areas of Asia, Africa, and Central America arrive at school not knowing how to use a pencil or eraser, virtually illiterate, and unable to perform basic computation in their native languages.

These students' transitions to regular classes are slow. Most take several years to gain a real working knowledge of English, and the complexity of secondary school materials also demands more language competence. Immigrants in junior high and high school typically take only physical education with native-born students in their first semester. By the end of the first year, however, many are taking standard English-language health and social studies classes.

Students who had made normal progress in their home-country schools can usually take regular mathematics courses within the first year, due to the relatively low importance of English expression and the fact that many foreign countries provide more demanding mathematics curricula. Students whose education has been disrupted by immigration often take much longer to catch up in secondary school. Few teenage immigrants who enter U.S. schools with deficient academic preparation ever make the transition to full-time English language instruction, and many leave school without diplomas and several years below normal grade levels.

The transcript analysis we conducted on a sample cohort of Los Angeles students illustrates students' experience in catching up with their U.S.-born age peers. The data are most vivid for immigrant high school students, over 25 percent of whom had entered U.S. schools at the high school level. We analyzed students' accumulation of credits in college-preparatory courses and their enrollment in algebra. These college-preparatory courses include algebra, geometry, laboratory science, history, and regular or advanced English, courses which are required for admission to the University of California and many other four-year colleges.

A comparison of Tables 3.4 and 3.5 shows that new immigrant tenth grade students in these schools lag behind all other students in the numbers of college-preparatory courses taken. By eleventh grade, however, the same immigrant students nearly catch up with their native-born and more established immigrant classmates. The percentage of new immigrant students who had not taken any college-preparatory courses fell from 44 percent to 22 percent between tenth and eleventh grade. By the end of their junior year, new immigrant students lagged only slightly behind the other two groups in the proportion taking more than six college-preparatory courses.

Immigrant students definitely catch up in the one important college "gatekeeper" course, first-year algebra. As Table 3.6 shows, new im-

Table 3.4

Percentage of Students Taking College-Preparatory Courses Through the 10th Grade

| Number of College Preparatory Courses | Type of Student | | |
	Native-Born	Established Immigrant	New Immigrant
0	35%	38%	44%
1–5	55%	46%	50%
6–10	10%	16%	6%
11–20	0%	0%	0%
N	20	37	18

Table 3.5

Percentage of Students Taking College-Preparatory Courses Through the 11th Grade

| Number of College Preparatory Courses | Type of Student | | |
	Native-Born	Established Immigrant	New Immigrant
0	25%	35%	22%
1–5	45%	32%	50%
6–10	15%	24%	22%
11–20	15%	8%	6%
N	20	37	18

Table 3.6

When Students Take First-Year Algebra

Percentage of Students Taking First-Year Algebra in	Type of Student		
	Native-Born	Established Immigrant	New Immigrant
Junior HS	15%	8%	0%
9th grade	25%	27%	28%
10th grade	15%	24%	17%
11th grade	0%	14%	39%
Never taken	45%	27%	17%
N	20	37	18

NOTE: The differences between groups are statistically significant at the 0.05 level.

migrant students take this course later than their classmates who were born in the United States or immigrated before they entered school. But the new immigrants are more likely than any other group in the sample schools to have taken algebra by the end of eleventh grade.

These data are only for immigrants who stay in school through the eleventh grade: The many who drop out before that time are unlikely to have taken any appreciable number of college-preparatory courses. Even those students who "catch up" in eleventh grade may have their college opportunities compromised. The standard college-preparatory sequence includes two years of algebra and one of geometry. Without taking summer school or delaying graduation by a year, the nearly 40 percent of new immigrants who start Algebra 1 in the eleventh grade would not be able to finish the entire sequence of courses.

Despite some positive results, educators in all the districts we studied reported that schools have great difficulty reaching and holding older students who enter school several years behind. They experience school as a struggle to catch up with courses that are continually moving faster than they can. Students who come from poor areas of their source countries often come from families that expect young people to abandon school in their teens to begin work and marriage. Many see the wages available even in dead-end U.S. jobs as being highly attractive, and some must take any available work to support their brothers and sisters. As a Chicago high school principal said, "The first [problem] area is attendance. Once a male is 16, he is expected to work. We have at least 300 kids here working more than 30 hours a week."

District officials and high school principals in San Francisco, Los Angeles, Fairfax, and New York said that older immigrant students are often too mature, and carry too many adult burdens, to participate in normal secondary school programs. Girls 13 or 14 years old may not be expected to earn money, but they may be responsible for maintaining the household and caring for younger siblings and cousins while their parents work several jobs. Boys of similar age may be expected by their families to work full time. Many of the children may have had experiences that forced them to permanently adopt adult perspectives. Aside from the traumatizing experiences associated with immigration itself, some children above the age of 14 may have served in regular or guerrilla armies and may have dealt daily with basic issues of life and death. This is most frequently true of young men from Central America, but it can also apply to immigrants from Cambodia, Afghanistan, and Kurdestan.

Few such students can adjust to the schedules and demands of regular high schools. In New York and Los Angeles, a small number of older immigrant students are enrolled in alternative schools, which offer flexible schedules and individualized programs. These were originally designed for U.S.-born students who were chronic truants, became parents, experienced emotional problems, or came under court supervision. These schools often work, in the sense that they help students continue their education and teach basic and interpersonal skills needed in adult life, but only a few students leave with a standard high school education.[3] Such schools are in very short supply. Many older immigrant students were also assigned to adult-education schools, where they could take advantage of flexible schedules and take a few classes at a time. Fairfax administrators who had worked with such students for several years said that the majority take only job-related vocational courses at first, but return

---

[3]The research on which these statements are based is reported in Hill, Foster, and Gendler (1990).

in their twenties to take more basic courses in English, mathematics, and economics.

Educators who are immigrants themselves consistently said that immigrant education is family education. Immigrant children generally do not attend school consistently or take all its demands seriously if their parents do not aspire to American-style education for their children. This is not a problem for middle-class immigrants from any country. But for the poor, the influence of traditional attitudes about children's roles in the family and aspirations for formal education is very strong.

Many school systems, especially San Francisco and Dade County, are working to make their class offerings more helpful and interesting to older immigrant students. But they, and educators in such other well-staffed school systems as Chicago, Houston, Fairfax, and New York, recognize that simply placing a student in a regular neighborhood school may not be enough for some immigrants. These districts have developed three kinds of activities that can supplement or strengthen regular instruction:

- *Newcomer schools* provide intensive language and academic remediation, assistance with social and emotional adjustment to the United States, health screening, inoculations, and remediation of chronic health problems.

- *Screening and intake centers* help schools by assessing new immigrants' English and academic skills, channel students into schools equipped to their needs, and allocate advisers and circuit-riding specialist teachers who can help schools educate students from low-incidence language groups.

- *Cultural adjustment programs* provide school-based courses intended to familiarize students with local history, politics, economic structure, geography, and cultural institutions.

Such activities are far from universal. Newcomer schools are present in all our California school systems and New York City. However, only Visalia has capacity in its newcomer school for a majority of new immigrants. Los Angeles has only two such schools and San Francisco four. Los Angeles serves only 5,000 of the approximately 30,000 newly arrived immigrant students who enroll each year. San

Francisco's newcomer schools can serve nearly 20 percent of newly enrolled immigrants. New York City has only one newcomer school, and it can serve only about 3 percent of each year's new arrivals. The California sites are committed to newcomer schools, and their availability is limited primarily by funding. New York might limit itself to the one existing newcomer school, because influential Puerto Rican groups complain that the school illegally isolates language-minority students from the mainstream.

Student Mobility.   Most schools are designed to provide nine months' instruction each year to students who start in September, leave in June, and return again in September. Los Angeles' year-round schools are a different but still very orderly and regular model. Within such stable schools, teachers can pass students from one grade level to another with some confidence that successive courses reinforce each other. Even when students transfer schools, curricula and standards are normally similar enough to permit students to adjust within a few weeks.

None of these assumptions holds for immigrant education. Immigrant children enter and leave school at times not normally contemplated by the school schedule, and they change schools frequently.

Districts with effective immigrant student intake centers assign students to schools on the basis of program, rather than location. In Dade and Fairfax, a family move does not automatically mean a change of school. Even if a student must change schools, the placement center can inform the new teachers about the student's needs and the program that had been created for her.

But four of our nine districts and, in all probability, the majority of all others, can provide neither the centralized placement service nor the transportation required to stabilize students' educational experience. In most districts, the majority of students enroll directly in their neighborhood schools and change schools every time the family moves. All school systems transfer records whenever a student moves, but a student's file normally arrives at the new school only after some weeks' or months' delay. Students' academic programs are often established before their records arrive.

Teachers and administrators cite other adjustment issues that particularly affect older students: the Latin cultures' expectation that
pregnant girls will leave school to raise their babies and that girls will
leave school to help their mothers; Southeast Asians' custom of early
marriages; and the expectations in most poor rural countries that
young men will become full-time workers in their late teens, and that
couples will marry and start having children before they are twenty.

If the experiences of other immigrant groups are standard, these
parental attitudes are unlikely to disappear until the second genera-
tion of immigrant children enters the schools. Although some
schools appear to have some capacity to increase family understanding and support, most do not. Some teachers and administrators
work to make their schools community centers, places where parents
can come to meet friends, get help translating documents, and enjoy
simple social events. These public schools become more than simple
purveyors of instruction; they are general resources for parents.
Their ultimate goal is to ensure parental support for the educational
process, but they approach parents by building community. Other
schools in our sample have tried to open themselves up as educational institutions, encouraging parent involvement in site-based
management and shared governance. Although these approaches
succeed occasionally, as in Chicago where Hispanic parents united
to have an Anglo principal removed and a Hispanic installed in his
place, immigrant parents in most schools do not respond.
Involvement with governance requires parents to shoulder additional burdens on behalf of the school (not, as in the former case, offering opportunities that parents themselves value). It also forces
immigrant parents to consider and decide on issues that most think
are the business of school professionals, not themselves.

Students' Adjustment to the United States. Teachers and principals
in every school talked about the emotional burdens borne by immigrant students, and the need to help. Most told about informal efforts by school staff to comfort grieving children and to help the most
destitute obtain clothing, food, and shelter. Most also expressed
frustration about the schools' inability to provide good counseling
and case management and about the remoteness and scarcity of
public-welfare resources. With a few exceptions (e.g., the close
working relationship between the Dade County Immigrant Student
Center and the Dade County Health Department), teachers and ad-

ministrators said they receive more help from private and religious charities than from public-welfare agencies.

Immigration has overloaded the health and welfare agencies just as it has the schools. And, like the schools, these agencies have received little additional funding despite their heavy new burdens. As Liu (1991) has shown, little of the funding promised health and welfare agencies under the Immigration Reform and Control Act of 1986 has materialized. Families are, moreover, likely to shy away from any but crisis help from such agencies. Although the schools have consistently demonstrated that they will serve children whatever their immigration status, many other public agencies are required by law to demand proof of eligibility for benefits.

Administrators and teachers in most schools perform part-time as surrogate nurses and social workers. In addition, some school systems also offer educational programs that help students learn to cope with the broader society and use its resources. The newcomer schools discussed above are meant to give students an intensive one-year adjustment to American life. In addition to individually tailored courses meant to help bridge any gaps between students' home-country education and U.S. courses, these schools teach students the rudiments of American manners, grooming, workplace deportment, and citizenship. According to the principal of Liberty High, New York City's one newcomer school, "these students need to know how the city works, how to get around, and how to deal with regular Americans. The school can't prepare them for everything but it can give them a start." The degree of help that is often necessary is evident in one New York City principal's statement:

> Some students come from rural areas and have never been in a city. These students are severely lacking in social skills. One had never been to school and didn't know how to hold a pencil, sit on a chair, or use a urinal.

Newcomer schools in California have much the same orientation. In some New York City comprehensive high schools, immigrant "houses" provide bilingual homerooms and rich social adjustment courses for some students.

Immigrant student intake centers also provide some help with adjustment. The ones in Dade and Fairfax counties ensure that immigrant students and their teachers get a weekly visit from a teacher, social worker, or consultant who knows the student's language and can provide advice, mediate disputes, or identify the need for intervention in family problems. Intake center resources are thin, and many grave needs may go unmet. But these resources are a distinct addition to the normal resources of the schools, which typically have only English-speaking counselors and only one for 300 to 500 students.

Table 3.7 shows which school systems have newcomer schools, intake centers, and programs geared to students' adjustment. A few school systems offer formal courses intended to help immigrant students learn about their new communities. Dade County's New Beginnings Program, which is intended for teenage immigrants who enter the schools without basic skills, also provides an orientation to the local community—its history, key institutions, main geographic features, labor market, and transportation opportunities. As explained by teachers in the Miami secondary schools, the program is not classroom-bound. Students visit key locations, are shown how to use public transportation, practice using newspapers and telephones, and are exposed to real cultural and work sites. Students in newcomer schools also get such experiences.

These experiences are time-consuming and have been criticized for taking students away from the important effort to gain basic reading and mathematics skills. Educators providing such programs counter that immigrants, especially older ones who may already be in the labor market and have responsibility for families, need these system-awareness skills. Students who learn to cope more smoothly with

Table 3.7

Special Programs Offered

Program	LA	SF	V	H	D	NY	C	F
Newcomer schools	X	X	X			X		
Screening & intake center	X	X	X	X	X			X
Cultural adjustment program		X			X			

neighbors, employers, and public-service providers may, in the long run, have greater freedom to develop basic and vocational skills.

Some individual teachers and principals in Houston, Chicago, and Fairfax provide such experiences at their own initiative. But in those school systems—as in Los Angeles and New York outside the newcomer schools—immigrant education is dominated by basic skills and language instruction.

The issue of whether schools should take responsibility for students' system awareness is an old one, and it is relevant to the education of native-born black and Hispanic students, as well as to immigrants. In other RAND studies of schools in Washington, Miami, Cleveland, Los Angeles, and New York, it is clear that disadvantaged urban youth of all races and ethnicities are strikingly ignorant of their areas' economic forces and civic and cultural institutions. Among a class of 15 seniors in one New York City high school, none had ever read a story in the *New York Times* and none could say what work was done on Wall Street or in midtown Manhattan. Less than half the freshmen in a moderately selective high school in Washington, D.C., could identify pictures of the Lincoln or Jefferson memorials or say what one might see when visiting the Smithsonian.[4]

The insularity of poor urban neighborhoods means that many native-born students are, in effect, immigrants as they cross into mainstream jobs and postsecondary education. Schools that address the acculturation needs of immigrant students may be pioneering a new and important element of education for all disadvantaged urban students.

UNMET NEEDS

The preceding sections can be seen as a catalogue of unmet needs— for more classroom space, bilingual teachers, books and curricula geared to the needs of specific immigrants groups, assessment centers and techniques, social services, and help with acculturation. This section relies on a special source of information, educators' re-

---

[4]The research on which these statements are based is reported in Hill, Foster, and Gendler (1990) and Hill and Bonan (1991). These particular findings have not, however, been previously reported.

sponses to our questions about what they are now trying to do to improve immigrant education, and what student needs are unmet.

We interviewed superintendents, school board members, central office administrators, teachers, and principals on this topic. Although responses differed from one person to another, there were no consistent differences associated with a respondent's job. All groups of respondents identified these needs:

- Efforts to integrate parents into the broader community, just as students are integrated via newcomer programs and social adjustment classes

- Better and more accessible adult education for parents and for older immigrant youth who cannot stay in high school

- Programs to reduce the hostility of some teachers who do not want to change their teaching methods to accommodate immigrant students

- Health care and screening

- Mentors for older immigrant students.

Parent Integration

Few communities have any organized way of helping immigrant adults learn about local opportunities and resources. Flawed though they may be, the schools are the only public agencies that consistently help immigrants adjust to their new lives. In areas where many immigrants are illegal, local community agencies are often closed and hostile to newcomer families.

Churches and established former immigrants perform "welcome wagon" services in the more stable and prosperous Cuban and Nicaraguan communities in Miami, in Asian areas of San Francisco, and in established Mexican-American areas of Chicago, Los Angeles, and Houston. But vast numbers of immigrant adults, especially those in areas that were traditionally occupied by Anglo-whites or African Americans, are left to fend for themselves. Our respondents thought that immigrant parents would more likely understand and support the demands of schooling if the broader community made a greater effort to accept and orient them.

Adult education is affected by the same budgetary crisis that has beset elementary and secondary schools. Whether adult education is funded separately, as in some of our districts, or jointly with elementary and secondary education, as in others, its budgets have been severely cut. Even in affluent Fairfax county, adult-education offerings have dwindled even as the demand for them has increased. Local adult-education enterprises in California grew dramatically during the rush to provide English classes for undocumented aliens who could be legalized under the Immigration Reform and Control Act. But those courses were temporary; funding and course offerings were dramatically reduced after the legalization program ended in 1990.

Respondents said that many older immigrant students cannot stay in regular high schools, but want to return for adult education in academic and vocational subjects. Many immigrant parents also try to take classes in English, simple mathematics, and vocational skills once they have gained some modest financial security. Opportunities for such coursework are, however, shrinking as the demand increases.

Immigrant adults, like the millions of native-born black and Hispanic adults who dropped out of high school but now see the need for further education, need courses tailored to their academic preparation and to their demanding schedules. If this need can be met, the elementary and secondary schools are likely to find that younger students benefit from their parents' greater understanding and support for schooling.

Improved Teacher Attitudes

It is a common belief that teachers of minority and immigrant children are more effective if they understand their students' home cultures. We expected our respondents to say that and were not disappointed. The vast majority of teachers and principals interviewed were dedicated to immigrant education and took delight in their contact with students. This was particularly true in schools that had traditionally served immigrants or had been restaffed once immigration brought a change in demographic composition. But there was active hostility on the part of some teachers. As teachers and principals in places as diverse as Los Angeles, Houston, Dade, and Fairfax told us, some of the more senior teachers, frequently the ones with tenure in a particular school, strongly resisted changing their course offerings or instructional strategies to accommodate the needs of immigrant students.

A Chicago principal recalled:

> I had a problem in the beginning with the faculty because they resented the idea of having their classes taught in any language but English. The departments also resented the extra help and money the classes for immigrant students received. This resentment has diminished almost completely through a lot of staff development workshops and faculty discussions.

The root of this problem is the change in neighborhood character brought about by the large influx of immigrants. In every district we studied, there were schools that had changed from Anglo or African American to immigrant Hispanic, Asian, or Caribbean. In a few cases, Mexican or Cuban Americans had been displaced by poorer immigrant Hispanics. While the school populations in those neighborhoods changed, the school staffs did not. Senior teachers with site tenure often chose to stay in convenient and comfortable surroundings, despite their lack of preparation for teaching non–English-speaking immigrants. Schools geared to providing compensatory reading and mathematics instruction to African American students had particular difficulty adapting.

Some school systems gave principals free hands to restaff schools that had not adapted to principals' needs. Others drove out recalcitrant teachers by ratcheting up standards for teacher effort and performance. But many school staffs, teachers and principals alike, continue to resent and resist the changes in familiar routines necessitated by "those children."

Many districts have initiated cultural awareness programs for teachers. Dade County, for example, is now devoting virtually all of its staff development budget to implementing the multicultural training elements of the META consent decree. Those programs cannot, however, work for teachers who do not want to change. In many districts, a serious collaboration between the central administration and the teachers' union is needed to staff immigrant schools with teachers who truly want to work in them.

Health Care and Screening

Teachers and principals in every city spoke of the need for health care. Many immigrant students from poor areas of Central America, Asia, or the Middle East have never seen a doctor or dentist or had an eye exam. Few have had the U.S. standard immunizations. Although school systems resist becoming comprehensive health-care agencies, they must prevent transmission of communicable diseases and seek help for students whose health problems make it impossible for them to attend school and learn. The consequences of inadequate health care for immigrants are causing serious problems in urban districts. For example, in 1989, Houston had the largest measles outbreak of any U.S. city (1763 cases, 266 hospitalized, and nine deaths). Medical experts attributed the outbreak to a combination of inadequate vaccines dispensed before 1979 and an influx of unimmunized immigrants. Similarly, the infection rate for tuberculosis among Houston school children rose to 5 percent in 1989, up from below 1 percent in 1984. Again, the problem has been attributed to the large influx of immigrants. Elementary school teachers in Dade County similarly reported that communicable diseases, and the disruption in student attendance that they cause, are major barriers to effective education.

Few city or county health departments offer strong programs of medical screening and care for immigrant children. Individual schools sometimes arrange special services from charitable organizations, hospitals, and medical schools. But few have access to such institutions, and many lack principals with the vast entrepreneurial skill and energy necessary to make such arrangements. School district central offices also lack the needed resources. For example, in July 1990, the Los Angeles district laid off all but three of its 50 doctors, and while 350 nurses continued to be funded, only high schools and some middle schools have them full time. Elementary schools in Los Angeles have nurses only one or two days a week.

As new immigrants come from increasingly impoverished and unsafe areas of the world, these problems will grow. But, as Liu (1991) shows, few general-purpose governments have organized to meet the needs of immigrant populations. Until this happens, schools facing profound educational challenges will also have to care for their students' health.

CHAPTER CONCLUSIONS

Six conclusions emerged from our district case studies.

First, the positive expectations that many educators hold for the immigrants they teach do not necessarily translate into appropriate and adequate services for those children. School systems accept immigrant students without asking questions about their immigrant status or family background. Many teachers and administrators in the districts we studied were themselves immigrants or children of immigrants. Many others are touched by immigrant children's eagerness and simplicity. But that does not mean that school systems have found ways to educate immigrant children successfully. School officials, from superintendents and school board members down to teachers and aides, are trying hard, at least in most cases, but they are not able to give immigrant children all they need to become full participants in American life.

Second, the school districts serving the largest numbers of immigrant students are deeply troubled and frequently fail to provide high-quality educational services to students of all sorts, including native-born, low- and middle-income children, as well as immigrants. Although the smaller districts in our sample, Fairfax and Visalia, were not particularly troubled, the big-city districts cannot meet their financial obligations, expect worse deficits in the years to come, are decades behind on building maintenance and reconstruction, and have severe shortages of classroom space, quality teachers, books, and supplies. The big-city districts are failing to educate a high proportion of their students—nearly half drop out before graduation in some cities—and some of the larger urban districts are unable to ensure the safety of students and teachers while in school.

Third, none of the districts have the kinds of assets normally considered necessary for the education of language-minority students. Although a few have adequate supplies of Spanish-speaking teachers, none can guarantee that immigrants speaking other languages will be taught by bilingual teachers. Even in wealthy Fairfax, some students never encounter a school employee who speaks their native language. In addition, many districts lack a capability to assess immigrants' language ability and general educational development.

Few districts have books, curriculum guides, or other instructional materials in any foreign language other than Spanish.

Fourth, shortages of teachers and instructional materials are not solely due to the school districts' financial straits. Many recent immigrant groups come from very poor regions, and few come to the United States with educated adults who can readily become teachers in U.S. schools. Further, except for Spanish-speaking students, there are few language-appropriate texts or materials that bridge the gap between educational approaches used in the United States and in source countries.

Fifth, some districts have explicit strategies for educating immigrants, but others do not. Districts with large, well-established foreign-language communities often regard immigrants simply as LEP students who need language instruction. This is true regardless of district wealth. Fairfax offers only ESL to foreign-born students, whether they are impoverished new immigrants or children of diplomats. However, districts whose LEP students are predominantly immigrants are much more likely to take responsibility for teaching students about how U.S. society differs from their native countries and how to cope with American school, work, and social situations.

Sixth, immigrant students, especially in the big cities, often appear in U.S. schools unprepared for the level of instruction normally offered students of their age. Older students have particular difficulty adapting. Family needs and pressures also frequently drive older students out of full-time school long before high school graduation. Educators expect such students to seek further education throughout their early adult lives, but few immigrant-impacted school systems are now equipped to provide it.

This chapter provides a picture of school districts coping with growing problems. Clearly, many districts and individual schools are making intelligent choices and showing great resiliency. But the big-city districts we studied, and many others like them, are failing virtually all their students—American-born blacks, Hispanics, and poor whites, as well as immigrants. And, despite the deficiencies of some individual principals and teachers, the main failures are systemic, not personal. Local governments have not taken responsibility for immigrant children's broader welfare or for helping their parents make a productive adjustment to American economic, civic, and educational life. State and federal governments have acted as if the problems brought about by immigration might just go away. The federal government, in an effort to promote general educational improvement, has ignored the fact that a few huge urban systems are near collapse and need special attention.

The theme of this chapter is also the dominant message of the entire report: For the vast majority of immigrant children, the quality of education depends on the fundamental strength and competence of big city school systems. The financial and educational weakness of those school systems impedes any effort to improve schooling for immigrant children.

Chapter Four

INSIDE IMMIGRANT SCHOOLS

In the previous chapter, we presented an overview of district efforts to meet the needs of immigrant students. To some extent, the responses of those local districts with the greatest numbers of immigrants are embodied in formal policies dealing with student assessment, the criteria for assigning students to particular schools, and the type of instruction they receive there. However, as the discussion in Chapter Three illustrated, much of what happens to immigrant youth is not the result of formal policies, but rather the sum of many different, ad hoc coping strategies by individual schools. Each school's unique response to bilingual teacher shortages, facility overcrowding, student mobility, and the myriad problems faced by poor immigrant families shapes the educational experiences of these students. Although all schools face the common challenges of teaching immigrants a new language, helping them adjust to a different culture, and teaching them needed academic skills, the educational experiences of students will vary depending on their age and level of past education, whether they speak Spanish or another language, and the type of school they attend.

In this chapter, we look inside several of the schools in our study sample to provide a more in-depth picture of immigrant students' schooling. It is meant to give greater specificity to the general discussion presented in the previous chapter and to show the variability in student experiences that can occur within the common set of challenges outlined in Chapter Three.

The most striking contrasts are between the traditional schools that most immigrant students attend and the newcomer schools available to a minority of students for a short period of time. Not only are the two types of schools quite different in their organization and approach to instruction, but the newcomer schools most closely approximate the restructured schools now being advocated by education reformers. In fact, these schools are exceptions to our larger argument about the fundamental incapacity of urban school systems. Newcomer schools are typically examples of educational institutions with a clear sense of mission, strong teacher professionalism, active links to other agencies serving children, and instruction customized to the unique needs of their clientele. Yet they are truly exceptions: They do not operate in all districts, and where they do exist, they serve a small minority of newcomers. Although resource constraints have prevented their expansion, they still represent an alternative vision of schooling for both immigrant and native-born students.

We first describe life for immigrant students in traditional schools, and then compare it with the experiences of those attending the newcomer schools in our sample.

TRADITIONAL SCHOOLS DOING THE BEST THEY CAN WITH WHAT THEY HAVE

Not only do the schools attended by most immigrant students have large enrollments, but they often have grown quickly. For example, one of the Houston elementary schools in our sample grew steadily over the 1980s, from 300 students in 1982 to over 1,000 by 1991. Similarly, schools in one of Chicago's immigrant neighborhoods are now about 25 percent over their physical capacity. One of the elementary principals in that neighborhood has been able to alleviate overcrowding for the close to 1,400 students attending that school only by renting unused classroom space in a nearby Catholic school. Even in rural Visalia, enrollment growth over the past decade has meant that half the elementary students attend school on year-round schedules, and the district expects to place the remainder on such a schedule over the next several years.

The fact that many immigrant students attend large, increasingly overcrowded schools affects the kinds of instruction they receive in several ways. First, the need to handle large numbers of students with limited teaching resources means that students tend to be homogeneously grouped, usually by language ability. For example, Dade schools group students by four levels of language ability; Chicago uses three levels; and Houston schools use five levels within their ESL programs. In some cases, these are within-class groupings; in other instances, students of different native- and English-language abilities are grouped in separate classrooms for at least part of the day. Because of the year-round schedule and the inability of schools to offer a full complement of courses on each track, grouping has taken on a new meaning in some Los Angeles schools. Students in one elementary school in our sample are placed on four different tracks: One track includes only gifted students, one is for Asians, and two are for Spanish-speakers. This arrangement was designed to maximize the efficient use of scarce resources. There are not enough qualified teachers to offer bilingual and gifted classes in each track, so teachers are matched with the students who most need them and are then concentrated in a particular track. The trade-off is that students' curricular opportunities are limited, and they are isolated from students of different language groups and abilities.

Not only are students grouped and isolated from one another, but also teachers often find it difficult to coordinate their efforts. The problem is particularly serious in high schools, where the ESL or bilingual component may be a small part of the overall curriculum. In some schools, isolation is also accompanied by disdain on the part of regular faculty toward the bilingual program. Even in schools where faculty would like closer ties between the LEP and regular curricula, however, barriers exist. For example, in several schools in our sample, overcrowding has meant that the ESL/bilingual students are taught in separate facilities, distanced from other students by several city blocks. Not only does this arrangement make social interaction more difficult, but it also thwarts efforts to ease the transition from bilingual to English language classes if LEP students cannot easily spend part of their day in the mainstream classes.

A second consequence of these fast-growing schools is the shortage of qualified personnel and the schools' consequent inability to offer the instructional programs either needed by students or required by state and federal statutes. For example, some Los Angeles LEP students receive what is called a "modified" bilingual program, even in the primary grades. Such a program usually means that they are taught by a monolingual, English-speaking teacher who is assisted by a bilingual aide. A Houston elementary school with close to 1,000 LEP students has only 20 teachers with bilingual certification and 13 with an ESL endorsement, so most LEP students above the third grade are placed in ESL classes. The school is able to maintain that number of bilingual teachers only by relying on long-term substitutes. In the case of Houston, the problem of providing sufficient access to bilingual classes is exacerbated by a state requirement that bilingual classes are to contain no more than 22 students.

Not only are the curricular opportunities available to immigrant and other LEP students significantly different from those for English speakers, but equally striking are the differences in academic course offerings for immigrant students themselves across districts, schools, and even within the same school. Three high schools in Houston, Los Angeles, and Chicago illustrate these contrasts. One-third of the students in the Houston high school are LEP. The school offers a full academic curriculum, including mathematics through honors calculus and science through honors physics, yet no bilingual classes are offered at all, and the only ESL classes available are in language arts. In the Los Angeles high school, located in a port-of-entry neighborhood, 45 percent of the students are recent immigrants, and two-thirds are LEP, speaking some ten different languages. This school is able to offer one college-preparatory course—biology—in Spanish. The only other bilingual courses are in remedial and introductory mathematics; U.S. and world history are offered in an ESL format. As a result, only students with sufficient English-language proficiency can take a full complement of college-preparatory courses. In contrast to the Houston case, however, about one-quarter of the teachers in the Los Angeles school are bilingual, so if students speak Spanish, Mandarin, or Tagalog, there is a high probability that, at least in some of their classes, teachers will be able to communicate with them in their native languages.

Course offerings for the one-quarter of students in the Chicago high school who are LEP (80 percent of whom are recent immigrants) stand in sharp contrast to those in the other two schools. Students whose native languages are either Spanish or Polish can take a college-preparatory curriculum that includes algebra, advanced algebra, geometry, biology, chemistry, physical science, geography, and

U.S. and modern world history taught in their native languages. Clearly, the curricular opportunities for newly arrived immigrants at this high school are greater than they would be if they attended schools in the other cities. But as impressive as this bilingual program may be, it does not serve the 40 percent of LEP students at the school who do not speak either Spanish or Polish. Those speaking Tagalog, Urdu, Rumanian, and some six or seven other languages can only be offered an ESL program without assistance from a teacher, aide, or tutor who speaks their language.

Variations in course offerings across these three schools are largely explained by the availability of bilingual teachers, but differences in state program mandates are also significant. The Chicago school has the program it does because state law, reinforced by a recent court decision, requires that schools offer a bilingual program in every language for which there are more than 20 students speaking that language. Texas law requires only that ESL classes be provided to high school students; while the intent in California is similar, there are currently no specific mandates in state law. These state mandates are not sufficient to ensure equal curricular access for immigrant students, but they do provide a legal framework, which then requires sufficient numbers of qualified teachers for successful implementation.

Both research evidence (e.g., McKnight et al., 1987; Oakes, 1990) and calls for school reform (Smith and O'Day, 1991) point to the importance of curricular access and academic content in shaping student achievement. Immigrants are not the only students whose schooling opportunities and experiences vary, depending on the schools they attend and the ability of those schools to accommodate their particular needs. But the problem is exacerbated in the case of immigrant students because they often attend schools that are rapidly growing and that can only make ad hoc adjustments in the face of quickly changing circumstances. Limited curricular access is most detrimental to older immigrant students who arrive in the United States in their mid-teens and have the ability and preparation to take college-preparatory courses, but lack English proficiency.

We have portrayed the schools attended by most immigrant students as institutions doing their best to cope given serious limitations of space, time, money, and faculty resources. Teachers with the training and experience to teach immigrant students are in short supply, and the typical counseling load in these schools is between 350 and 500 students. Other support services, such as those provided by medical and mental-health personnel, are available only on an irregular and limited basis.

But it is important to note that, within this general picture of schools trying to make do under difficult circumstances, there are examples of valiant efforts to be innovative and to make a significant difference in the lives of students. Schools in Dade, Chicago, Los Angeles, and other districts are moving to site-based management; some are working to develop a more integrated, thematic curriculum; and a few are implementing parental education programs to help parents become more effective teachers of their children. The problem is that these efforts are often sporadic, and many are limited to one school or even one grade level or academic department within that school. These are not the systemic changes that will be necessary to improve schooling for both immigrant and native-born children.

In the next section, we examine one strategic approach to immigrant education that may serve as a model for improving urban schooling more generally.

NEWCOMER SCHOOLS: A NEW MODEL FOR IMMIGRANT EDUCATION

The first difference one notices between the newcomer schools in our sample and the traditional ones is size. For example, the two newcomer schools in Los Angeles each enroll about 450 students, as compared with the other Los Angeles elementary schools in our sample, which average over 1,000 students, and the high schools, which typically enroll between 2,000 and 4,000 students. But other differences are also evident. Because newcomer schools were created as "new" schools,[1] their mission is well-articulated and clearly

---

[1]Although newcomer schools are new organizational entities, they tend to be housed in existing buildings. For example, the newcomer elementary school in Los Angeles is housed in a building that was originally a neighborhood elementary school in the city's wealthiest neighborhood. Immigrant students are bused from the central city to this sylvan setting, which stands in sharp contrast to their own neighborhoods. The Los Angeles newcomer high school operates as a "school-within-a-school" at a high

manifested in their organization and curriculum; the faculty members are usually handpicked, based on their expertise and willingness to work with newcomers. Perhaps because they are viewed as different by district authorities or perhaps because they are headed and staffed by a self-selected group of educators, newcomer schools also tend to operate more autonomously and to involve staff more directly in school governance. These schools, by virtue of the clientele they serve, also tend to establish stronger links with community agencies.

The defining characteristics of newcomer schools are well-illustrated in Visalia's newcomer elementary school, which is now in its third year of operation, serving about 115 newly arrived immigrant students in grades three through six. The teachers were all handpicked by the district's bilingual coordinator, who also served as the first director of the school.[2] The school is a close-knit, caring community where the teachers have designed the curriculum and decided which instructional materials to purchase. It has an easygoing, egalitarian atmosphere. The aides eat lunch with the teachers; much of the conversation revolves around the children and school activities; and the aides' suggestions are treated equally with the teachers'. As an example of the emphasis on caring and developing a positive self-image, each child receives a gift and card from the school on his or her birthday. Then, once a month, the school has a birthday party, and all children with birthdays in that month receive their own cakes. The school's aides spend four hours a day in instructional tasks and three hours outside the classroom assisting students and parents— e.g., driving children to the doctor, bringing parents to the school.

The objective of the newcomer school is to help immigrant students experience success and thus develop a positive self-image and to

---

school located in one of the city's working- and middle-class black neighborhoods. The newcomer center in Visalia is housed in a small rural school located next to a county-run migrant labor camp that local legend identifies as one of the camps where Steinbeck gathered material for *The Grapes of Wrath*.

[2]Despite the experience and skill of the teachers selected for the newcomer center, only one currently has a bilingual credential. Two have language development credentials, and two are working on their bilingual credentials. The school's resource teacher, a young Latino male who is being groomed to become principal of the newcomer school, also has a bilingual credential. He works with the teachers and aides at the newcomer school and also with the ESL teachers at two of the middle and high schools in our study sample.

gain a firm foundation in English-language development. The whole curriculum is based on giving students a lot of hands-on experience (e.g., through the use of field trips about once a month, hands-on science projects, writing in journals). The entire curriculum is designed around seven general themes: self, family, community, county, state, country, and world. Within each of these units, content strands are covered in science, mathematics, social studies, language arts, health, art, music, and physical education. The organizing principle for the curriculum is the school's own design, but the faculty relies heavily on textbooks based on California's state curriculum frameworks. In contrast to the curriculum in most traditional elementary schools, this one is well integrated across subject matter and grade levels and is the topic of ongoing discussion and consultation among the teachers.

Because of the lack of bilingual teachers in the Southeast Asian languages, instructional strategies differ at the Visalia newcomer center for Spanish-speaking and Southeast Asian students. The Spanish-speaking students are taught for half the day in their native language, while the Southeast Asian students are taught entirely in English using language development techniques. They are organized in two classes by language group and can work with the aides in their native languages.[3] For example, mathematics is largely taught by the aide in the students' native language. In the afternoon, the Southeast Asian and Hispanic students are combined for English-language instruction. These classes are organized thematically (self, family, community, etc.) according to the school's curriculum framework, with each afternoon spent concentrating on a different subject (one day each for social studies, art, literature, math, and science).

Because of its small size and the scope of services provided, the newcomer center costs more to operate than a typical school. Some of these additional costs are borne by the local district, and others are supported with federal and state funds. The major additional costs include the use of five aides who work seven hours daily (these are funded by federal Title VII and state compensatory education funds),

---

[3]Actually, not all the language groups can speak with an aide. In one third-through-sixth-grade class, the students speak three different languages. The aide speaks two of those languages; the older Hmong students translate for the others; and the aide also speaks Thai, which some of the children learned while in the refugee camps.

small class sizes (22 as compared with the district average of 32), transportation costs, and Spanish-language materials. The last three costs are borne by the district.

The other newcomer schools in our sample reflect a similar climate and approach to instruction. For example, one of the newcomer schools in Los Angeles enrolls students in the fourth through eighth grades. Like the Visalia school, it places a strong emphasis on building student self-esteem; the faculty was handpicked by the principal and participates actively in making decisions about curriculum, the school calendar, and the use of school resources. Like other schools in the district with predominantly minority student bodies, the average class size in this school is about 27, as compared with close to 35 in many of the district's other schools. Students do much of their classwork in mixed-ability, cooperative groups.

This school also has more support personnel than a typical elementary or middle school in the fiscally strapped district. It has a full-time nurse, a full-time counselor, part-time student attendance and adjustment counselors, and a part-time psychologist. But even this augmented staff is insufficient to meet the needs of students beset with the emotional problems of separation and poverty. However, the school has been fortunate in securing the volunteer services of psychiatrists from UCLA and one of the large local hospitals. Some of these psychiatrists are bilingual, and their services are in such great demand that the principal has used a lottery to determine which classrooms will receive assistance. The school also has volunteers from the local community who work with students several days a week, and several philanthropic organizations provide clothing, eyeglasses, and some medical services. Because the school is so far from where most students live, the principal and a group of teachers hold a meeting for parents one evening a month at an elementary school in the neighborhood where most of the students live. Attendance averages about 30 to 100 parents a month, and the school tries to present programs of interest to parents on such topics as gang prevention. School staff members also make home visits, and a district van is available to bring a limited number of parents to the school for conferences.

There are two newcomer high schools in our sample—in Los Angeles and San Francisco. Both schools are about the same size and comprise Latino and Asian students, with Latino students the majority in the Los Angeles school and Asians in San Francisco. The educational levels of these students vary greatly, ranging from the preliterate to those working considerably above grade level. In the Los Angeles school, about 50 percent enter at the ninth-grade level with grade-level skills in their native languages; about 10 percent are preliterate and receive a full bilingual program; and the remaining 40 percent have skill levels in their native languages somewhere between the fourth and seventh grades. Skill levels are somewhat higher in the San Francisco school because of the presence of more affluent students from Hong Kong. But most of the students come from poor and troubled backgrounds. In the Los Angeles newcomer school, many students are not living with both their parents; some served in the El Salvadoran army or experienced other traumas; and about 5 percent are homeless at any given time.

The curriculum in the newcomer high schools stresses both student adjustment to new surroundings and achievement in academic subjects. The first objective is pursued much as it is at the lower grade levels, through language development, orientation courses, field trips, and hands-on experience (e.g., students in the Los Angeles newcomer school are matched as pen pals with native-born students in the regular school taking Spanish as a foreign language). Because these schools are able to recruit a higher proportion of bilingual teachers, more academic subjects are taught in students' native languages than is typical in most California high schools. Among the 17-person faculty in the Los Angeles school are teachers who speak Spanish, Cantonese, Mandarin, Tagalog, French, and Arabic. In the San Francisco school, students are placed in mathematics classes by language group with, for example, Cantonese speakers able to take courses up through calculus from a native speaker. Social studies courses are taught as ESL classes, but the social studies department chair is a former member of the Peace Corps who speaks Thai and Laotian. Even keyboarding is taught by a Cantonese teacher, assisted by a Spanish-speaking aide and a Chinese-speaking electrical engineer from Pacific Bell, who volunteers three hours a week to help students develop leadership and interview skills and who also takes them on field trips to the downtown area. However, because students only stay in the newcomer schools for a year or less, the opportunity to take vocational courses, particularly ones taught bilingually, is quite limited.

Teachers in the newcomer high schools also tend to pay greater attention to curriculum development than do those in traditional schools. Part of the reason stems from the need to adapt the curriculum to a constantly changing student body that may differ from year to year in students' countries of origin and academic skill levels. But the philosophy of newcomer schools, with its dual emphasis on cultural acclimation and academic achievement tailored to a wide variety of skill levels, means that the curriculum is more integrated across academic subjects than is typical in most high schools. The emphasis on building student self-esteem also leads teachers to rely more on such techniques as cooperative work groups and portfolio assessments.

Like the newcomer schools serving the lower grades, the high schools have more counseling resources than traditional schools, but they still need more than can be supported by district funds. However, because newcomer schools are seen as innovative and meeting an important need in their communities, they can often obtain resources from private businesses, foundations, and local community organizations. For example, the work of the two full-time counselors at the San Francisco newcomer school is supplemented by counseling interns from San Francisco State University and counselors from a Latino and a Vietnamese community organization.

CHAPTER CONCLUSIONS

The newcomer schools in our sample are impressive places: In their clear sense of mission, innovative curricula, professional teaching staff, and links to the larger community, they represent the kinds of schools to which all children, immigrant and native born, should have access. However, several factors prevent them from being declared an unqualified success. First, they only serve a minority of immigrants and for only a short period (one year in most cases, six months in San Francisco). The reason for their limited availability is cost. Smaller school and class sizes, a higher ratio of support personnel, field trips, and a richer mix of instructional materials mean that these schools can cost anywhere from several hundred to over a thousand dollars more per student.[4] Without a significant change in school funding, such additional expenditures are highly unlikely in today's fiscal climate.

Second, civil rights groups have questioned the appropriateness of segregating immigrant students for even six months to a year. Ironically, then, some immigrant advocates are calling for more new-comer schools and for ones that allow children to stay for up to several years, while other groups would like to see them abolished. This same issue has arisen in Holland, France, Britain, and Germany, with concern expressed in all four countries about the isolation of "reception classes" for immigrant students. Because there is now a growing consensus that students need to be integrated into regular classes as soon as possible and that those classes should be prepared to receive them, newly arrived students in France and Germany continue to attend reception classes but are simultaneously assigned to regular classes where they spend part of their time (Glenn, 1992).

Finally, there have been no systematic evaluations comparing those students who have attended newcomer schools with those who have not. Part of the problem is that such districts as Los Angeles do not yet have the means to track students after they leave the newcomer schools.[5] However, as more student records become computerized, systematic assessments of student experiences after they leave the

-----

[4]The newcomer schools in our sample are all self-contained programs that students attend full-time for one or two semesters, and all but the Los Angeles high school operate in physically separate locations. However, there are a variety of other newcomer models, including ones that students attend for half a day and then spend the remainder of the day in mainstream classes. In contrast to the schools in our sample, in which students from across a district are transported to a single site, some districts, such as Long Beach, operate newcomer classrooms on as many as a dozen different campuses. For a description of these other program models, see Cheng (1990).

[5]One of the frustrations of faculty at the elementary/middle newcomer school in Los Angeles has been that not only is there no systematic way to track their students once they leave, but efforts to keep these students together have been unsuccessful. The principal and teachers had hoped to have all the students assigned to a middle school with a strong bilingual/language development program located close to the newcomer school, so that the faculties at the two schools could consult regularly about students as they continue their studies. The district has not accommodated that request, but the faculty is still working to prevent newcomer students from being dispersed around the district.

newcomer centers will be possible. Until then, the success of these schools can only be judged by the fact that they are clearly schools where students like to be and by some limited evidence about short-term effects. For example, because the newcomer high school in Los Angeles is located within a comprehensive high school, it can track its former enrollees who choose to remain at that school. Of the students from the school's first year of operation who stayed at the comprehensive high school, 55 percent earned a B average or better, and 80 percent of the honor students in the regular high school program were former newcomer students.

As with much of public education today, there is a certain "luck of the draw" quality to the schooling available to immigrant students. Within a broad framework of some language development, academic instruction, and limited support services, students' opportunities and experiences can differ significantly, depending on the school to which they are assigned. Schools start with different resource levels and some cope more creatively and effectively than others, but the end result is to infuse the education of immigrant students with considerable variation. Although they too are constrained by the limited supply of bilingual teachers, newcomer schools provide a more focused alternative that ensures recent immigrants fortunate enough to be enrolled in them with a richly integrated educational experience, at least for a short time.

Chapter Five

IMPROVING IMMIGRANT EDUCATION

We began this report by arguing that immigrant education is best understood as a policy with diffuse benefits and concentrated costs. Policymakers, scholars, and the general public disagree about the relative costs and benefits of immigration, but there is widespread agreement that the costs are heavily concentrated. Because these costs fall overwhelmingly on a few states and local districts, most notably in California, the rest of the country has little incentive to concern itself with the education of immigrants.

The argument that concentrated costs make immigrant education a low-visibility issue seems to have even more validity now than it did some three years ago when we began this study. The most recent example of national policy failing to address immigrant needs came in September 1992 when a congressional conference committee decided to strip $812 million in previously approved federal funding from health and education programs for newly legalized immigrants. Former Rep. Edward R. Roybal (D-Calif.) explained why the funding was not appropriated; "I blame it on the fact that California is really the only state suffering the consequences of this" (Bunting, 1992). Not only has California spent close to $350 million more on the newly legalizing population than it received from the federal government (one of only three states to do so), but the expenditures unreimbursed by the federal government now equal considerably more than the state's reserves.

The further retreat of the federal government from assisting in the education of immigrant students could not come at a worse time for the states and local districts serving these students. Not only are such states as California, Florida, and Texas fiscally battered, but a seriously weakened economy, growing social problems, and the heightened political rhetoric accompanying these conditions will make it harder and harder for states and localities to mount special programs for immigrant students. One need only consider the arguments of California's Republican governor that immigrants are among the "tax receivers" the state can no longer afford to subsidize so generously, public opinion polls showing that the overwhelming majority of respondents consider immigrants to be more of a burden than a benefit, or a recent essay in a liberal magazine arguing that

> If and when free higher education for immigrants, especially illegal immigrants, comes under attack, however, free elementary and high school education for them will almost inevitably come into question as well. And the social dislocation lurking in the latter question is almost incalculable. (Miles, 1992, p. 62)

In this fiscal and social climate, it is no surprise that the federal government and most state governments are reluctant to mount large-scale programs tailored specifically to the needs of immigrant students.

Yet these students cannot be ignored. They represent an increasing proportion of the students enrolled in urban schools, and they will constitute a key segment of the future labor force. These students also challenge schools in paradoxical ways. On the one hand, our research and a number of other studies indicate that immigrant youth are remarkably successful in school. Yet the dropout rate for Latino youth is twice what it is for Anglos, and research has found that recent immigrants are more likely to drop out of school than other students, even controlling for other relevant factors (Rumberger, 1991). Similarly, the educational and social needs of immigrant students are much like those of native-born students attending urban schools, but they also have unique needs that include, but are not limited to, English-language acquisition, cultural adjustment, and remedying the effects of limited formal education. The challenge for those working on behalf of immigrant students is to ensure that their unique needs are addressed at a time when they enjoy little attention at the national level and are in danger of attracting negative attention in some localities.

In this final chapter, we confront that challenge by combining two themes that emerge from this study. The first has already been mentioned: the low visibility of immigrant education in most policy circles and its relegation to the good intentions and coping strategies of individual districts and schools. The second is the recognition that the greatest barrier to quality education for immigrant students is an overall lack of basic capacity in urban school districts. We argue that two kinds of recommendations must flow from this study. Certainly, strategies need to be promoted that are specific to improving the educational outcomes of immigrant students. However, we believe that the most effective way to improve schooling for immigrant students is to enhance the overall capacity of urban school systems. Not only does attacking the broader issue of comprehensive school reform make sense educationally, but it is also more likely to have wider political appeal. Rather than being seen as a California or a Florida problem, systemic reform of urban education can be viewed as a policy in which large numbers of people throughout the country have a stake. In this way, assistance to immigrant students can be transformed from a policy with concentrated costs into one in which costs and benefits are shared by many.

MEETING THE UNIQUE NEEDS OF IMMIGRANT STUDENTS

We first identify needs specific to immigrants that can no longer be met effectively by individual districts and schools working in isolation. Investment by all levels of government and by the public and private sectors alike is critically needed in four areas. The first is the recruitment and training of bilingual teachers. Scholarly and political debates over how long language-minority children should remain in bilingual classrooms or what instructional strategies should be used there are no more than hypothetical exercises as long as bilingual-teacher shortages remain so acute. Most educators and policymakers familiar with the needs of LEP students would agree that they require sustained contact with teachers who speak their native language, at least for some initial period. But as our study has indicated, many recent immigrants—particularly older students and those speaking low-incidence languages—either have no contact with school personnel who speak their language or only with aides. Although it is a long-term strategy, the most effective one for increasing the supply of bilingual teachers is to give bilingual instructional aides the opportunity to become teachers. Some school districts, in cooperation with local universities, are mounting such training programs. The university offers undergraduate and teacher-training courses at satellite facilities close to the schools where aides work; the district gives the aides paid leave time to attend classes and, in some cases, finds practicing teachers who will serve as tutors and mentors. Certainly, providing incentives for monolingual English teachers to learn another language remains an important strategy, but training able immigrants is more likely to produce teachers who speak low-incidence languages (particularly the Southeast Asian ones) and has the added advantage of providing immigrant students with role models from similar backgrounds. For these programs to produce significant numbers of bilingual teachers, however, a broader effort will be required than can be mounted by any single higher education institution or school district. Ideally, the effort should be a coordinated, statewide one that includes multiple universities and school districts and is supplemented with significant amounts of student financial aid. Particular attention should be given to increasing the supply of well-trained subject-matter teachers (particularly in mathematics and science) who are also bilingual.

A second area of needed investment is instructional support, including the development of textbooks, curriculum frameworks, and student assessments. Although better materials are needed in Spanish, the most acute needs are in lower-incidence languages, for which textbook and testing publishers have no financial incentive to produce materials. Several types of investment are possible. In some cases, materials can be purchased from the countries to which a particular language is indigenous, but in others, new materials will have to be developed in the United States. One strategy for doing that might be collaborative projects between university foreign-language and area centers and schools of education. In this way, language proficiency and cultural expertise can be linked with subject-matter, curricular expertise. Language proficiency and academic achievement tests are also nonexistent in languages other than English and Spanish. Often schools must rely on informal assessments conducted by aides who have no formal training in student assessment techniques, and study respondents expressed concern about the reliability and validity of these informal efforts. The federal government might, as part of its research and development function, fund such development as collaborative activities among foreign language and area centers, private test developers, and university-based testing and measurement experts.

In the previous chapter, we discussed newcomer schools and their potential benefit to newly arrived immigrants. The additional cost associated with these schools makes it unlikely that their numbers will substantially increase in the near future. However, modified versions, such as schools-within-schools, reception classes that students could attend for part of the day, or a cultural orientation curriculum that can be integrated into the regular academic course of study, may be more feasible with modest levels of additional support. In addition, as part of the broader education-reform movement discussed in the last section, schools are likely to have more of an incentive to differentiate their approaches to instruction depending on the types of students they serve. More schools with a newcomer orientation may emerge under such a system.

The third and fourth areas of needed investment are ones that would assist poor students generally, but have particular relevance to immigrants. One is greatly expanded adult-education programs. One of the most frequent responses given by principals and teachers to a question about services most needed by immigrant students was that greater educational opportunities for parents would translate into more successful schooling for children. When they talked about adult education, respondents mentioned English-language instruction, high school equivalency classes, vocational training, and workshops on effective parenting. But demand for adult education has far outstripped supply over the past decade, and enrollment in most of the adult education programs in California is now capped. Although the shortfall is not as acute in other states, districts serving large numbers of immigrant students need greater capacity to provide a variety of adult education classes.

Finally, there is a pressing need for coordinated delivery of educational, health, and social services and the provision of such services by those familiar with the language and culture of immigrant children. Few of the schools in our sample have routine, easy access to the support services often desperately needed by their students. The return of previously eradicated diseases, such as measles and tuberculosis, to Houston and Los Angeles points to the need for preventive health care that can be delivered through the schools. As one Los Angeles school board member noted in discussing reductions in school health personnel, "today, we need school nurses for far more important things than scraped knees." It is those nurses, counselors, and school psychologists who can serve as the bridge between schools and outside institutions such as other government agencies, community organizations, and medical schools.

Substantial investment in these and other strategies to assist immigrant students is unlikely to occur until there is a significant change in how the education of immigrant students is viewed politically. Until there is a stronger consensus about the level of societal benefits derived from immigration and whether those benefits should be viewed as national in scope, there will be little incentive for national policymakers to assist the states and localities most affected by the costs of educating immigrant children.

BUILDING LOCAL CAPACITY

The need to change in a fundamental way how national policymakers view students in big-city schools applies not just to policies for immigrant youth. It also lies at the core of the second set of recommendations that flow from our research and from that of many other studies of urban education.

Though there are many federal and state programs intended to improve the education of students disadvantaged by poverty, disability, or minority status, none address the basic problem of low organizational capacity in local school systems. Since the enactment of the Elementary and Secondary Education Act of 1965, the vast preponderance of federal funding for education has been directed toward services for specific disadvantaged groups. Federal categorical programs have assumed that a school system's basic programs are sound and effective for the majority of students, but that local educators do not focus sufficient attention on the needs of disadvantaged students. Federal programs single out disadvantaged students for additional help, subsidizing the creation of specialized administrative units, provision of special instructional services, and the hiring of teaching staff dedicated to providing these services. The core assumption of all such programs is that public schools are adequate for the majority of students, but that disadvantaged students need "something extra."

The conditions identified in this study do not match that core assumption. None of the urban districts we studied is able to provide effective services for the majority of its students. Only a narrow segment of middle-class students, normally concentrated in magnet schools and isolated neighborhood enclaves, can be expected routinely to stay in school through twelfth grade, graduate on time, and be prepared for higher education or rewarding work. In the larger cities, the majority of students are members of minority groups that federal programs have singled out for special treatment. However, because federal programs are structured to supplement a basic instructional program that is assumed to be adequate, they do nothing to remedy the inability of local systems to provide a sound educational program for the majority of their students.

Today's most widely discussed reform, the national education goals and the standards movement initiated by the Bush administration and now endorsed by the Clinton Administration, address the problems of typical American school districts. They focus on the need to raise aspirations and standards, ensure that children enter school prepared for learning, and encourage greater accountability. Many state reform programs have a similar character. They assume that school systems have the money necessary to improve their own performance, if only efforts are properly focused by means of goals, standards, and accountability measures. Current reform proposals do not contemplate the creation of new curricula for students who cannot profit from full-time instruction in English, nor do they remedy the shortages of teachers and texts that can provide a bridge between immigrant students' native languages and English.

By failing to address the needs of the urban districts that enroll many immigrant students, current reform efforts overlook a major threat to our national well-being. The problems of these districts are geographically localized: Most of the failing districts are surrounded by suburban and small town districts that are doing reasonably well. But the size and economic importance of the great urban districts are such that the threat of their simultaneous collapse would jeopardize the future of whole states and, ultimately, the nation.

A few simple figures illustrate the importance of these districts. According to Hodgkinson (1992), Hispanic immigrant and African-American youth will provide more than half of the net growth in the U.S. labor supply in the early 21st century. Those students are dramatically concentrated in a few places. The Hudson Institute estimates that 40 percent of all African Americans of school age live in eleven central cities. The Census Bureau estimates that nearly 75 percent of all Hispanic immigrant children, and children born to recent Hispanic immigrants, reside in five major metropolitan areas. These areas overlap with the eleven containing 40 percent of Blacks, and all are included in this study: Los Angeles, Miami-Dade, Houston, New York, and Chicago. Together, these five cities educate nearly 1 in 20 American students of elementary and high school age.

Today's reforms may be appropriate for the majority of U.S. school systems that are reasonably solvent, well staffed, and able to provide appropriate services to the majority of their students. They may also be of some value to smaller urban school systems that serve a stable native-born population, particularly one with a fair representation of middle-class students, whether black, Anglo, or Hispanic. But the basic elements of today's reform agendas do not address the core problems of the large urban districts. They do not provide funds to relieve overcrowding and reconstruct dilapidated school buildings, point the way to renewal of failing schools with jaded or poorly trained staffs, create a new supply of teachers who can speak immigrant students' home languages, or develop curriculum materials that take full account of students' academic preparation.

Because of their size and disproportionate importance in educating critical elements of tomorrow's adult population, the giant city school systems are of national, not just local, importance. They are too devastated to improve by themselves, and the consequences of neglecting them will not be limited to the metropolitan areas or the states in which they are located.

The Need for National Action

Enhancing the capacities of big-city school systems is a national problem. As custodian of the national economy (and as manager of the foreign and national security policies that often stimulate immigration), the federal government surely has responsibilities in this area. But other state and national institutions also have important interests and competencies. The effort to improve the capacities of big-city school systems must engage state and local governments, universities, and foundations, as well as the federal government.

Federal and state governments face two challenges. First, they must find a way to focus resources on the big cities. Most current programs spread benefits as widely as possible, and in doing so ignore the distinctiveness of the big cities. Federal and state categorical programs send a high proportion of their funds to the cities, but these funds are targeted for services to particular students, and those services are about the same in cities as in suburban or rural areas. Nothing about such programs is tailored specifically to urban problems or is flexible enough to increase general capacity when that is, in fact, the problem. The second challenge for the federal and state governments is to find ways of helping the big cities improve their school systems across the board. In the past, the federal government has been especially leery of general aid to school systems, fearing that unconstrained grant funds might be used to abate local taxes or improve schooling for the children of wealthy, influential parents, not the poor. Those fears are not unrealistic, but some way must be found around them. Federal and state grants—perhaps governed by city-specific contracts specifying allowable uses, outcome expectations, and renewal contingent on performance—are the only possible sources for the amounts of money needed to upgrade urban education.

In claiming that current national reform proposals do not go far enough in addressing the needs of urban students and that more fundamental capacity-building is required, we are not arguing against the various reforms now being advocated under the banner of school restructuring. In fact, the discussion of newcomer schools in the previous chapter illustrates the effectiveness of three major components of school restructuring—site-based management; an integrated, thematic curriculum; and stronger links between schools and community institutions.[1] Site-based management establishes the principle that schools can differ from one another and that

---

[1]For an overview of the major components of school restructuring and their underlying assumptions, see McDonnell (1989).

school staff should tailor programs to the changing needs of students. Site-based management also gives those closest to students the authority to make curricular and personnel decisions. Those advocating curricular reform most often justify it in terms of giving all students equal access to rigorous coursework and a schooling experience integrated across subject areas and between the academic and the practical. But little attention has been paid to adapting these principles to the needs of language-minority students. The contrasting curricula of newcomer and traditional schools, however, suggest that such an effort would be beneficial for immigrant students. As noted in the previous section, strengthening the links between schools and community agencies is a pressing need in all urban schools, especially those serving immigrants.

Nevertheless, despite the appropriateness of school restructuring strategies for urban students, it is important to consider two points. The first relates to another major aspect of school restructuring—greater accountability for educational outcomes through student standards and assessment strategies with significant consequences. We have already alluded to the shortcomings of an approach that rewards and punishes schools when students have only limited access to relevant curricula and when valid assessment instruments are unavailable. But there is a larger issue that needs to be kept in mind when considering greater accountability for urban schools. Accountability implies a reciprocal relationship between schools and the broader community. Schools are to produce educational outcomes desired by the community, but in return, the community needs to provide the legitimacy and support to make those outcomes possible. In its highest form, accountability is a social contract—an acceptance of shared responsibility between schools and the larger society. Consequently, an emphasis on greater accountability will not result in more effective learning for urban students if the community retreats from its side of the bargain. Civic officials, business leaders, other public and private agencies, and the general public must do more than press for greater accountability; they must also take active responsibility for the education of all the children living in their city.

The second point is simply a restatement of one made several times in this report. In its ideal form, school restructuring implies a fundamental redesign of schooling—changes in organization and governance, curriculum, relationships with the larger community—and it assumes that the entire system will change, not just a few schools in the most innovative or affluent communities. In practice, however, school restructuring has typically moved in piecemeal fashion—e.g., site-based management implemented with no changes in curriculum, new forms of assessment without retraining teachers. It has also tended to be implemented in individual schools and through small-scale projects, unconnected to the systems of which they are a part. Such an approach will not solve the problems of urban schools. The school restructuring movement can improve learning outcomes for a majority of urban students only if it is comprehensive in its application and if it is aimed at rebuilding the basic infrastructure of urban school systems.

CHAPTER CONCLUSIONS

From our vantage point 100 years later, we can question the effectiveness of the education reforms prompted by the last major wave of immigration, and the ethnocentrism that motivated them. But there may be one important lesson we can learn from that period. At that time, the education of immigrant children was not viewed as a problem to be ignored. The progressive reformers, no matter how misguided they may seem now, saw the changing composition of urban schools as an opportunity for a fundamental transformation of the U.S. education system.

It would seem that with the benefit of a century's learning, policymakers today might well change their perspective and redefine this newest wave of immigration as another opportunity for profound change. Small categorical programs and ad hoc local responses have their place, and certainly immigrant children could benefit from better services specific to their unique needs. But their chances for a productive and satisfying life will only truly be enhanced if the system that educates all students in large city schools is greatly strengthened.

Aronowitz, M., "Adjustment of Immigrant Children as a Function of Parental Attitudes to Change," *International Migration Review,* Vol. 26, No. 1, 1992, pp. 89–110.

Aronowitz, M., "The Social and Emotional Adjustment of Immigrant Children: A Review of the Literature," *International Migration Review,* Vol. XVIII, No. 2, 1984, pp. 237–257.

August. D., and E. E. Garcia, *Language Minority Education in the United States,* Springfield, Ill.: Charles C. Thomas, 1988.

B. W. Associates, *Meeting the Challenge of Language Diversity: An Evaluation of Programs for Pupils With Limited Proficiency in English*: Vol. II, *Findings and Conclusions* (R-119/2), Berkeley, Calif.: B. W. Associates, 1992.

Borjas, G. J., *Friends or Strangers: The Impact of Immigrants on the U.S. Economy,* New York: Basic Books, Inc., 1990.

Bunting, G. F., "Congress Cuts Aid Proposed for Immigrant Care," *The Los Angeles Times,* October 2, 1992, p. A3.

California State Department of Education Task Force on Selected LEP Issues, *Remedying the Shortage of Teachers for Limited-English-Proficient (LEP) Students,* Report to the Superintendent, 1990.

Callahan, R. E., *Education and the Cult of Efficiency,* Chicago: University of Chicago Press, 1962.

Caplan, N., J. K. Whitmore, and M. H. Choy, *The Boat People and Achievement in America: A Study of Family Life, Hard Work, and Cultural Values*, Ann Arbor, Mich.: University of Michigan Press, 1989.

Castaneda v. Pickard, 648 F.2d 989, 5th Cir., 1981.

Chambers, J., and T. Parish, *Meeting the Challenge of Language Diversity: An Evaluation of Programs for Pupils With Limited Proficiency in English: Vol. IV: Cost of Programs and Services for LEP Students* (R-119/4), Berkeley, Calif.: B. W. Associates, 1992.

Chang, H. N., *Newcomer Programs: Innovative Efforts to Meet the Educational Challenges of Immigrant Students*, San Francisco: California Tomorrow, 1990.

Cheung, O. M., and L. W. Solomon, *Summary of State Practices Concerning the Assessment of and the Data Collection About Limited English Proficient (LEP) Students*, Washington, D.C.: Council of Chief State School Officers, 1991.

Crawford, J., *Bilingual Education: History Politics Theory and Practice*, 2nd ed., Los Angeles: Bilingual Education Services, Inc., 1991.

Cremin, L. A., *Popular Education and Its Discontents*, New York: Harper and Row, 1990.

Duran, B. J., and R. E. Weffer, "Immigrant's Aspirations, High School Process, and Academic Outcomes," *American Educational Research Journal*, Vol. 29, No. 1, 1992, pp. 163–181.

Fass, P. S., *Outside In: Minorities and the Transformation of American Education*, New York: Oxford University Press, 1989.

Fass, S. M., *The Hmong in Wisconsin: On the Road to Self-Sufficiency*, Vol. 4, No. 2, Milwaukee: The Wisconsin Policy Research Institute, 1991.

GAO—see U.S. General Accounting Office.

Glenn, C. L., "Educating the Children of Immigrants," *Phi Delta Kappan*, January 1992, pp. 37–40.

Gomez v. Illinois State Board of Education, 811 F.2d 1030 (7th Cir. 1987.

Hakuta, K., *Mirror of Language: The Debate on Bilingualism*, New York: Basic Books, 1986.

Hill, P. T., and J. J. Bonan, *Decentralization and Accountability in Public Education*, Santa Monica, Calif.: RAND, R-4066-MCF/IET, 1991.

Hill, P. T., G. E. Foster, and T. Gendler, *High Schools With Character*, Santa Monica, Calif.: RAND, R-3944-RC, 1990.

Hodgkinson, H. L., *A Demographic Look at Tomorrow*, Washington, D.C.: Institute for Educational Leadership, 1992.

Hull, E., "Undocumented Alien Children and Free Public Education: An Analysis of Plyler vs. Doe," *University of Pittsburgh Law Review*, Vol. 44, No. 2, 1983, pp. 409–432.

Johnson, W. B., and A. Packer, *Workforce 2000*, Indianapolis: Hudson Institute, 1987.

Lau v. Nichols, 414 U.S. 563, 1973.

McCarthy, K. F., and B. R. Valdez, *Current and Future Effects of Mexican Immigration in California*, Santa Monica, Calif.: RAND, R-3365-CR, 1986.

McDonnell, L. M., *Restructuring American Schools: The Promise and the Pitfalls*, presented at the Conference for Education and the Economy: Hard Questions, Hard Answers, sponsored by the Institute on Education and the Economy, Teachers College, Columbia University, 1989.

McDonnell, L. M., L. Burstein, O. Ormseth, J. M. Catterall, and D. Moody, *Discovering What Schools Really Teach: Designing Improved Coursework Indicators*, Santa Monica, Calif.: RAND, JR-02, 1990.

McGroarty, M., "The Societal Context of Bilingual Education," *Educational Researcher*, Vol. 21, No. 2, 1992, pp. 7–9.

McKnight, D., F. J. Crosswhite, J.A. Dossey, E. Kifer, J. Swafford, K. J. Travers, and T. J. Cooney, *The Underachieving Curriculum,* Champaign, Ill.: Stipes Publishing, 1987.

Miles, J., "Blacks vs. Browns," *Atlantic Monthly,* October 1992, pp. 41–68.

National Coalition of Advocates for Students, *New Voices: Immigrant Students in Public Schools,* Boston: NCAS Immigrant Student Project, 1988.

New York State Education Department, *Status Report on Certification and Licensing of Bilingual and English as a Second Language Teachers in New York State: 1986–1990,* New York: Division of Bilingual Education, 1990.

Oakes, J., *Multiplying Inequalities: The Effects of Race, Social Class, and Tracking on Opportunities to Learn Mathematics and Science,* Santa Monica, Calif.: RAND, R-3928-NSF, 1990

Ogbu, J. U., "Minority Status and Literacy in Comparative Perspective," *Daedalus,* Vol., No. 2, 1990, pp. 141–168.

Olsen, L., *Crossing the Schoolhouse Border: Immigrant Students and the California Public Schools,* San Francisco: California Tomorrow, 1988.

Plyler v. Doe, 102 S. Ct. 2382, 1982.

Ravitch, D., *The Troubed Crusade: American Education 1945–1980,* New York: Basic Books, 1983.

Rumberger, R., "Chicano Dropouts: A Review of Research and Policy Issues," in R. R. Valencia, ed., *Chicano School Failure and Success: Research and Policy Agendas for the 1990s,* New York: The Falmer Press, 1991, pp. 64-89.

Schmidt, P., "Faced with lawsuit, Florida revamps education for language-minority pupils," *Education Week,* Vol. 10, No. 1, September 5, 1990, p. 31.

Shuit, D. P., and P. J. McDonnell, "Calculating the Impact of California's Immigrants," *The Los Angeles Times,* January 6, 1992, pp. 1, 19.

Simon, J., "Immigrants, Taxes and Welfare in the United States," *Population and Development Review,* Vol. 10, No. 1, 1984, pp. 55-69.

Smith, M. S., and J. O'Day, "Systemic School Reform," in S. H. Fuhrman, and B. Malen, eds., *The Politics of Curriculum and Testing,* Bristol, Penn.: The Falmer Press, 1991, pp. 233–267.

Stanfield, R. L., "Melting Pot Economics," *National Journal,* Vol. 24, No. 8, 1992, pp. 442–446.

Suárez-Orozco, M. M., and C. E. Suárez-Orozco, *Hispanic Cultural Psychology: Implications for Education Theory and Research,* paper presented at a workshop on immigrant children in California schools, Center for U.S.-Mexican Studies, University of California, San Diego, January 23, 1993.

Suárez-Orozco, M. M., *Central American Refugees and U.S. High Schools.* Stanford, Calif.: Stanford University Press, 1989.

Tyack, D. B., *The One Best System: A History of American Urban Education,* Cambridge, Mass.: Harvard University Press, 1974.

U.S. Department of Education, *The Condition of Bilingual Education in the Nation: A Report to the Congress and the President,* Washington, D.C.: Department of Education, Office of the Secretary, 1991.

U.S. General Accounting Office, *Immigrant Education: Information on the Emergency Immigrant Education Act Program,* GA/HRD-91-50, Washington, D.C., 1991.

Valverde, S. A., "A Comparative Study of Hispanic High School Dropouts and Graduates: Why Do Some Leave School Early and Some Finish?" *Education and Urban Society,* Vol. 19, No. 3, 1987, pp. 320–329.

Willig, A. C., "A Meta-Analysis of Selected Studies on the Effectiveness of Bilingual Education," *Review of Educational Research,* Vol. 55, No. 3, 1985, pp. 269–317.

Wilson, J. Q., *Bureaucracy: What Government Agencies Do and Why They Do It,* New York: Basic Books, 1989.